W9-BRG-255

COINS

JOHN PORTEOUS

 OCTOPUS BOOKS

The author wishes to thank Dr C. H. V. Sutherland, Mr Philip Grierson and Mr Ian Stewart for their encouragement and criticism, and Miss Gillian Wright for her help in collecting the illustrations. He also wishes to thank Mademoiselle J. Lallemand of the Bibliothèque Royale de Belgique, Mr Graham Pollard of the Fitzwilliam Museum, Cambridge, Dr F. Panvini Rosati of the Istituto Italiano di Numismatica, and Monsieur J. Yvon of the Bibliothèque Nationale, Paris, for their kind help with the selection of coins for the colour illustrations. The author also thanks the following people who have given him assistance with several illustrations: Miss J. M. Trafford, E. K. Cox Esq, Monsieur J.-M. Nicaud, N. G. Rhodes Esq, Dr Roberto Rocchigiani and J. D. A. Thompson Esq.

The author and publishers with to thank the following collectors who have made available coins from their collections: Philip Grierson Esq, figures 73, 76 (the coin of Louis the Pious), 82, 93. Figures 36, 43, 76 (the coins of Cuthred and Coenwulf), 134, 177, 184 are of coins in the Westminster School collection, made available by kind permission of the Head Master. The author wishes to record his special gratitude to Messrs P. & P. Santamaria, Rome, who, at an early stage in his writing the book, placed at his entire disposal the whole set of plates of one of their sale catalogues. Figure 183 was specially photographed for this book by the International Nickel Co (Mond) Ltd.

The following illustrations are reproduced by coutresy of the authorities, directors, keepers and curators of the following museums, companies and institutions: the Administration des Monnaies, Paris, figures 70, 131, 144, 181; the Archivio di Stato, Siena, figure 83; the Heberden Coin Room, the Ashmolean Museum, Oxford, figures 2, 6, 7, 8, 25, 28, 32, 59, 61, 67, 71, 72, 75, 85, 86, 88, 104, 106, 112, 119, 122, 138, 141, 142, 148, 149, 150, 153, 154, 155, 157, 158, 163, 171, 175; A. H. Baldwin & Sons Ltd, figures 162, 165, 169; Bank Leu & Co AG, figures 27, 57, 120, 121; the Bibliothèque Nationale, Paris, the jacket, figures 1, 20, 90, 109, 132, 137, 176; the Bibliothèque Royale de Belgique, Brussels, figures 11, 12, 17, 19, 99, 108, 125, 126, 129, 146; the British Museum, figures 3, 4, 5, 9, 13, 14, 15, 16, 18, 21, 22, 23, 29, 33, 34, 38, 41, 47, 49, 52, 54, 62, 63, 64, 65, 66, 80, 94, 102, 114, 116, 143; the Fitzwilliam Museum, Cambridge, the endpapers, figures 76 (the coins of Offa) 164, 166; the Rheinisches Landesmuseum, Trier, figure 60; the International Nickel Co (Mond) Ltd, figures 160, 161, 162, 167, 169, 170, 174, 179, 180, 183; the Istituto Italiano di Numismatica (Collection of King Victor Emmanuel III), figures 107, 123, 124, 130, 139; Le Mans Cathedral, figure 95; the Musée du Louvre, Paris, figure 117; the National Historical Museum and Royal Coin Cabinet, Stockholm, figure 151; the National Portrait Gallery, London, figures 147, 182; the Österreichische Nationalbibliothek, Vienna, figure 128; the Royal Mint, London, figures 105, 152, 160, 170, 174; P. & P. Santamaria, figures 10, 24, 26, 30, 31, 37, 39, 42, 44, 45, 46, 48, 50, 55, 56, 58, 69, 77, 92, 106, 111, 113, 115, 133, 136, 140, 145, 172, 173; Jacques Schulman NV, figure 135; the Schweizerisches Landesmuseum, Zurich, figures 68, 74, 89, 118; SPADEM, figure 95; Spink & Son Ltd, figure 178; the Staatliches Münzkabinett, Berlin, figures 35, 40. Figures 78, 79, 8¹, 87, 91, 96, 97, 98, 101, 103, 127, 159, 168 are from the author's collection.

The following illustrations were obtained from the following sources: Archives Photographiques, Paris, figure 84; the Deutsches Archaeologisches Institut, Rome, figure 51; Editions Argra, Toulouse, figure 100; the Mansell Collection, London, figure 60.

Figures 11, 12, 19, 99, 108, 125, 126, 129, 146 were photographed by Paul Bijtebier; figure 95 by the Compagnie des Arts Photomécaniques; figures 34, 114, 116 by Fine Art Engravers Ltd; figure 117 by Giraudon; figure 83 by Cesare Grassi; figures 35, 40, 53 by Hirmer Verlag; figures 90, 131, 132, 156 by Christiane Meurisse; figures 107, 123, 124, 130, 139 by Oscar Savio; figures 36, 43, 73, 76, 78, 79, 81, 82, 91, 93, 96, 97, 98, 101, 103, 127, 134, 159, 164, 165, 166, 168, 177, 178, 184 by Derrick Witty.

This edition first published 1973 by
OCTOPUS BOOKS LIMITED
59 Grosvenor Street, London W1

ISBN 0 7064 0048 8

© 1964 George Weidenfeld & Nicolson Ltd

Produced by Mandarin Publishers Limited
77a Marble Road, North Point, Hong Kong
and printed in Hong Kong

Preceding page
8 louis d'or, 1640
Louis XIII [enlarged about 4 : 1]

CONTENTS

4

COINS OF THE GREEKS

2 Lydia, electrum $\frac{1}{3}$ stater, seventh century BC, on the reverse a simple punch mark; the lion's head was the badge of the Mermnads, the first dynasty to issue coins [actual size].

3 Lydia, silver siglos (shekel), Croesus (561–546 BC); Croesus was the first ruler to establish coinage in gold and silver [actual size].

4 Persia, gold daric, Darius, c. 515 BC; these coins were struck until Alexander's conquest of Persia in the fourth century BC [actual size].

1 (opposite) Bactria, 20 staters, c. 160 BC, Eucratides. The biggest ancient gold coin in existence; on the reverse the king is described as basileus megalos (maharajah) [twice actual size].

'LYDIA,' WRITES HERODOTUS, 'unlike some other countries, does not present many wonders worth describing, except the gold brought down from Mount Tmolus.' The Lydians, like their neighbours the Ionian Greeks, were a trading people short of land for agriculture but well placed for commerce between the uplands of Anatolia and the sea. Their gold provided them with a ready means of exchange and, according to Herodotus, they became the first shopkeepers.

Gold and silver had long been used in trade, and perhaps as early as 2500 BC the Babylonians had invented a system of weights; but it was only about the seventh century that, according to one theory, Ionian merchants, who found themselves repeatedly weighing and testing the same lumps of metal, thought of marking them so that they would know them again. At first a mere punch mark was enough, but, as the marks of respected merchants came to be accepted in houses other than their own, something more recognizable was needed. It was discovered that, if the surface on which the metal was placed was engraved with a personal device, the lump would receive, as it were, a seal's impression on the other side when the punch was driven home.

Coinage is issued for the public account, whereas the Ionian merchants seem to have stamped their pieces for their own purposes. The decisive step in the evolution of coinage was taken by the kings of Lydia in the seventh century BC. Like most kings, they controlled the production of precious metals in their territory and they found it both profitable for themselves and convenient for the trading community to issue metal from the royal treasury, already weighed and guaranteed, stamped with the royal badge, the lion's head of the Mermnad dynasty [figure 2].

The original coinage of Lydia was made of electrum, the natural alluvial alloy of gold and silver found locally, which then commanded its own price without reference to its variable gold and silver content. As the king monopolized the supply, he controlled the market, but no specific denomination of value seems ever to have been attached to the primitive Asiatic electrum coinage. Indeed the Ionian cities of Phocaea, Cyzicus and Mytilene, which continued to issue artificially compounded electrum coins until the middle of the fourth century BC, always put them on the market for what they would fetch.

5 Syracuse, silver decadrachm, *c.* 479 BC, believed to have been struck by the tyrant Gelon after his victory over the Carthaginians in 480 BC; there may be a likeness to his queen, Demarete, in the features of Arethusa [enlarged about 3 : 1].

That the Lydian kings effectively controlled their market is suggested by the decision of Croesus (561–546 BC), the last and most famous of them, to abandon electrum for a dual coinage of gold and silver, valued on a fixed ratio of $13\frac{1}{3}$:1. As this was a tiresome ratio for daily transactions, he reduced the size of the gold coin to make it ten times the value of the silver [figure 3]. The bimetallic system was taken over by the Persians when they conquered Lydia, and late in the sixth century a currency of gold *darics*, named after King Darius, [figure 4] and silver *sigloi* (shekels) was instituted for the Persian Empire. Both gold and silver bore the image of the Great King with a bow in his hand, a type which remained virtually unchanged until the Alexandrine conquest. One and a half darics a month per man was the agreed pay of the Ten Thousand for their part in Cyrus' expedition against Artaxerxes in 401 BC and fifty darics the price of Xenophon's horse when he was obliged to sell it at Lampsacus on the way back.

Before the invention of coinage, the Greeks of the mainland had used a currency of iron and copper spits *(obeloi),* six of which made up a handful or *drachma*. According to one chronicler, the early seventh-century tyrant Pheidon of Argos abolished this currency, substituting for it one of silver; but the first coins in the area are those of Aegina and they seem to date from about 625 BC. Aegina, situated in the Saronic gulf between Argos and Attica, was a prosperous trading community, and in the island of Siphnos it controlled a plentiful supply of gold and silver. It took as its badge the sea-turtle, which abounds in its off-shore waters [figure 7] and, as its credit was good and the 'turtles' had

6 Caulonia, silver stater, *c.* 550–470 BC (the fabric is the same as figure 9); Apollo was the patron god of Caulonia [twice actual size].

6

7 Aegina, silver stater, *c.* 600 BC; the 'turtles' were the earliest coins of Greece and dominated Aegean trade in the sixth century [actual size].

8 Corinth, silver stater, *c.* 550 BC; the archaic letter *koppa*, initial of Corinth, appears under the body of Pegasus [actual size].

9 Croton, silver stater, *c.* 550–470 BC; this illustrates the curious fabric of coins of Magna Graecia at that time, with the obverse design repeated on the reverse, but incuse [twice actual size].

the obvious advantage that in Aeginetan territory they had a fixed value of two drachmas each, this coinage dominated Aegean trade during the seventh and sixth centuries.

Corinth, the chief trading community west of the isthmus, was the next major Greek city to issue coins, probably about 575 BC. She was in no position to challenge Aegina on her own ground, as her silver supply was far up the Adriatic and the metal was therefore dearer at Corinth than at Aegina: the Corinthian *stater,* current at three drachmas, weighed not much more than two-thirds the Aeginetan, which was current at two drachmas. Nevertheless Corinth had her own trading area westward, up the Adriatic and across it in Magna Graecia, and there her coins found acceptance; they were known as 'colts' from the device of Pegasus, the winged horse which Bellerophon had captured on Acrocorinthus [figure 8].

The earliest 'colts' had a simple punch mark on the reverse like the coins of Aegina, but the Corinthians developed the idea of cutting another intaglio design in the punch so that the coin received an impression on both sides. The design chosen for the stater was the patron goddess of the city, Pallas Athene, wearing a helmet of Corinthian style. The advantage was not only aesthetic: by changing the reverse design it was possible to differentiate between denominations, taking Pallas for the stater and bareheaded Aphrodite for the drachma, while preserving Pegasus intact, as the badge of Corinth, on them all. Before that Pegasus had been chopped up on the smaller pieces.

While Corinthian staters circulated freely in Magna Graecia, the cities there also frequently recoined them on their own account. The early one-sided Corinthian coins were difficult to restrike without cracking, but the Greeks of southern Italy

10 Acragas, silver tetradrachm, fifth century BC, reverse [twice actual size].

11 *(left to right)* Macedon, tetradrachm, Perseus (179–168 BC); Seleucid Kingdom, tetradrachm, Antiochus III, the Great (223–187 BC); Bactria, tetradrachm, *c.* 190 BC, Antimachus. Perseus was the last king of Macedon before the Roman Conquest, and Antiochus another and more powerful enemy of Rome; Antimachus is known only from his coins [actual size].

invented a new technique to give such restrikes extra strength. They engraved the reverse die in relief to produce an incuse impression on the coin; the designs on the two sides were the same but reversed, and the two dies were aligned on the same axis. This technique, which produced the effect of repoussé work, has been ascribed to Pythagoras who migrated to Croton in the latter part of the sixth century; it was abandoned soon after the Corinthians adopted thicker two-sided coins. The designs were very handsome, typical of their period in their bold simplicity: a tripod for Croton [figure 9], a bull looking back for Sybaris, an ear of barley for Metapontum, and statues of Apollo and Poseidon, the patrons of Caulonia [figure 6] and Poseidonia.

The owl had been a badge on Athenian coins since about 575 BC, but the 'owls', unlike the 'colts' and the 'turtles', were not at first important as a trading currency. The sea route east of Athens was blocked by Aegina, 'the eyesore of the Piraeus', and in any case the Athenians, who like the Corinthians had to import silver, could not compete with Aegina in the same market. However, the increase in the power of Athens and the discovery of silver at Laurium in Attica during the sixth century quite changed the situation, and in about 525 BC, in the time of the

12 Gela, silver tetradrachm, *c.* 440 BC, reverse; on this coin the Syracusan motif of Arethusa and the dolphins is adapted to the river god of a neighbouring city [enlarged 4 : 1].

tyrant Hippias, a new and larger coin of four drachmas, the *tetradrachm,* was introduced. After 480 BC, when the Persian War had established Athens as the foremost city in Greece and the discovery of more silver deposits in Attica had made her even richer, the new coinage supplanted the Aeginetan as the main currency of the Aegean. It had a high reputation and hoards of Attic tetradrachms have been found as far away as Spain and the banks of the Oxus. The Athenian democracy made somewhat tyrannical use of its new power and did its best to put an end to autonomous silver coinages within its sphere of influence; the 'turtle' coinage, which was a point of special jealousy, was suppressed from 456 BC until after the Peloponnesian War.

On the Athenian coinage of 525 BC the owl was transferred to the reverse of the coins and a head of Athene was put on the obverse, which gave her more pride of place than she enjoyed

9

13 Athens, silver tetradrachm, c. 510 BC [twice actual size].

14 Athens, silver tetradrachm, after 480 BC; Athene's laurels may commemorate the victories of the Persian War. Compare the conscious archaism of the style with figure 13 [twice actual size].

15 Eretria, silver tetradrachm, early fifth century BC; obverse cow, reverse cuttlefish [twice actual size].

at Corinth. Some of the early heads of Athene on these tetradrachms, the eye set full-face in the profile head, as on early bas-reliefs and vase-paintings, are among the most charming of early Greek coins [figure 13]. This was the first time that human features had been given such prominence on a coin, and it seems that the Athenians were very proud of their pieces, so proud indeed that they could not bring themselves to change them later. After about 480 BC a laurel wreath was conferred on the patron goddess, perhaps in commemoration of the victories of Marathon and Salamis [figure 14], but then there was virtually no change for two hundred years, and as late as 250 BC the Athenian coinage was still struck in a degenerate archaic style. In spite of the sentimental attachment of the Athenians towards their old-fashioned coins which is revealed in the comedies of Aristophanes, this conservatism owed something to fear of the damage which a change in the appearance of the coinage might

10

16 Olympia, silver didrachm, *c.* 450 BC; [twice actual size].

17 Aetna, silver tetradrachm, *c.* 480 BC; the dies for this unique coin are thought to be by the same master as those of the Naxos tetradrachm, figure 18 [twice actual size].

18 Naxos, silver tetradrachm, *c.* 470 BC; as a centre of the wine trade Naxos put the head of Dionysus and the figure of Silenus on its coins [twice actual size].

do to its credit. The Athenian was the first of many important international coinages to crystallize in this way.

In the years which followed the appearance of the first Attic tetradrachms and the two-sided Corinthian staters, many Greek cities took up the issue of coins. For some it was perhaps no more than a gesture of independence, but for others it satisfied a genuine economic need, as in the case of Olympia, for example, which was the centre of a great fair at every Olympic festival. Die-engravers had by this time some generations of experience in representing animals on coins, but with human forms they were still unpractised. The former they achieved with great skill and directness of vision: the crab [figure 10], one of the badges of Acragas in Sicily, minutely observed in all the subtle planes of its shell and the cunning articulation of its joints, and the cow [figure 15], on coins of Eretria in Euboea, which scratches its nose with its hoof in a gesture you can almost hear. Human features were still regarded with a certain awe, such conventions as the profile eye and the archaic smile distorting the natural vision to reveal the ideal qualities of the soul. Nor was this style unsuited to features which were after all not those of men but of gods. Its most successful exponent was the Aetna master, who made dies for Naxos in Sicily about 470 BC. Naxos was a centre of the wine trade and its coins show the head of the city's patron, Dionysus [figure 18]. About ten years earlier the same engraver had achieved a remarkable synthesis between this numinous quality and animal realism in his portrayal of Silenus on a coin of Aetna. The satyr's brutish but lively features and the big beetle below his neck are offset by the elegance of the reverse, Zeus at ease on his throne, nonchalantly toying with a thunderbolt [figure 17].

19 *(left)* Thrace, tetradrachm, *c.* 300 BC, Lysimachus; *(right)* Pergamum, tetradrachm, *c.* 240 BC, Attalus I. The earliest Greek coin portraits were posthumous: Lysimachus honoured his master, Alexander the Great, and Attalus his uncle, Philetaerus, who ruled Pergamum until 263 BC [enlarged 3:1].

The passionate interest in the human figure, which artists developed in the years after the Persian Wars, was soon displayed on almost all Greek coins except those of Athens. This interest received its purest and most formal realization in central Greece, notably in the figures of Nike [figure 16] and in the profiles of Zeus which appeared on coins of Olympia. In the west, however, and particularly in Sicily, it found a freer and more various expression.

When other cities of Sicily had taken for their badges such creatures as the crab and the cock, Syracuse, still governed by an oligarchy, had chosen a four-horse chariot, reflecting perhaps the expensive tastes of her ruling class [figure 5]. The Syracusans never lost, indeed they developed, their early feeling for elegance, and after the fall of the oligarchs they still kept their

handsome device, which, as the city's influence spread, was much copied in Sicily. As a design for the reverse, Syracuse took the profile head of Artemis Arethusa and soon adopted the convention of surrounding her with dolphins to symbolize the city's most arresting natural feature, a freshwater spring surrounded on three sides by the sea [figures 5 and 27]. Like the chariot, this happy idea was developed by later artists, and was often imitated, for example, by neighbouring Gela, whose patron river-god was surrounded by three fish [figure 12].

On coins of Magna Graecia and Sicily the nymphs are all pretty, the gods benevolent and the horses thoroughbred. Even those

13

23 Egypt, copper coin of Cleopatra VII (48–30 BC), mint of Alexandria; a late example of Hellenistic portraiture which belies the legend of the queen's beauty [actual size].

24 Leontini, silver tetradrachm, c. 466–422 BC [actual size].

25 Thurium, silver tetradrachm, c. 410 BC [actual size].

21 (opposite left) Egypt, silver tetradrachm, c. 300 BC Ptolemy Soter; a god in his own kingdom after the tradition of the Pharaohs, Ptolemy was the first living man whose portrait appeared on a coin [enlarged 3 : 1].

22 (opposite right) Catana, silver tetradrachm, c. 415 BC, from dies engraved by Heracleidas [enlarged about 3 : 1].

of the most severe style [figure 24] have a sensuousness which is usually absent from coins of the Greek mainland, except perhaps those of Corinth, the most luxurious of the Greek cities and the mother of Syracuse and many other colonies. If the spirit, however, was Corinthian, the workmanship was frequently Athenian and it was perhaps this infusion of Attic salt which preserved the coins from too much sweetness and mere prettiness.

How handsome later Athenian coins might have become had the style at home been allowed to evolve, may be guessed from the coinage of Thurium and Velia, Attic colonies in Magna Graecia [figure 25]. These are coins of strictly Athenian type, but marked by the artistic developments of the later fifth century. In Sicily, whither many artists fled after the plague of Athens in 430 BC, engravers seem to have been given a freer hand. Their work was much prized, and as they were permitted to sign their dies, we know some of their names: Euainetos, Cimon, Heracleidas and Eucleidas. Euainetos and Cimon both engraved dies for a series of large decadrachms struck at Syracuse after 413 BC to mark the victory over the Athenian expedition and subsequent victories over the Carthaginians. These artists, who worked in very high relief, gave to the profile head of Arethusa and the racing chariot their final and most magnificent interpretation [figure 33]. Cimon, Heracleidas and Eucleidas also achieved the most difficult task of the die-engraver, the successful portrayal of the facing head. Cimon at last showed the Syracusans the full face of the charming Arethusa; Eucleidas, perhaps gilding the lily, crowned her with the Medusa helmet of defeated Athene; finally, Heracleidas, for tetradrachms of Catana, made a magnificent head of Apollo, glaring and shimmering like the midday sun [figure 22].

As a series, the coinage of Sicily in the hundred and twenty years after 480 BC has never been surpassed, whether for design or technique, but the most beautiful of all coins of this time was made in the Persian Empire at the Ionian city of Clazomenae, by an engraver signing himself Theodotus [figure 20]. By 360 BC the facing-head convention was widespread and the full face of Apollo was the standard type for the coinage of Clazomenae. It is interesting to compare Theodotus' treatment of this subject with that of Heracleidas fifty years earlier. The Catanian Apollo dazzles us with his eyes and fiery hair. Theodotus conveys an impression of equal power and cruelty by the subtle forms of Apollo's brow and lip, without recourse to picturesque effects.

During the Peloponnesian War the Athenians, cut off from their silver supply, resorted to a plated coinage, which made their tetradrachms shabbier than ever in contrast to the coins of Sicilian and other mints. A less disreputable expedient, which was adopted not only by the Athenians, but also by the Syracusans in their emergency, was coinage in gold, which had until

26 Macedon, silver tetradrachm, Philip II (359–336 BC); obverse head of Zeus, reverse jockey who recalls Philip's victory at the Olympic Games [actual size].

then rarely been issued outside the Persian Empire. The first to challenge the Persian position was Philip II of Macedon, who began his career of conquest by encroaching upon the independent tribes of Thrace and the cities of the Chalcidian League. The barbarians of Thrace took little part in international trade, but their mines were among the richest of the ancient world and they had been accustomed to issue large silver coins from late in the sixth century [figure 28], most of which were later recoined to the standards of the great trading cities. Philip's control of these Thracian mines contributed largely to the spread of his political influence throughout Greece. He coined according to two standards, the Thracian for silver and the Attic for gold, both

27 Syracuse, silver tetradrachm, c. 450 BC, reverse [twice actual size].

28 Acanthus (Macedon), silver tetradrachm, c. 520 BC; the tribes of northern Greece exploited their rich silver mines from late in the sixth century [twice actual size].

29 Egypt, silver tetradrachm, c. 305 BC, Ptolemy Soter; one of the earliest of all portrait coins: Alexander wears the elephant skin of an eastern conqueror, and the ram's horn of Ammon curls over his temple [twice actual size].

30 Olynthus, silver tetradrachm, c. 392–358 BC [actual size].

31 Macedon, gold stater, Philip I (359–336 BC) [actual size].

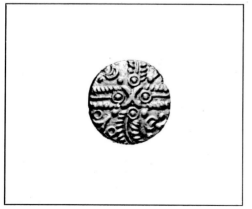

32 Britain, gold stater, c. 50 BC [actual size].

inherited, together with the profile head of Apollo as the obverse type of the gold, from the conquered Chalcidian city of Olynthus [figures 30 and 31]. The reverse of Philip's gold was a chariot and that of the silver [figure 26] a race-horse, devices recalling his own name and his victory in the Olympic Games of 356 BC.

Philip's gold supply was so plentiful that he was able to coin it in a price ratio to silver of only ten to one, and his staters soon superseded the more expensive darics as the standard gold currency of the ancient world. As late as 197 BC they formed a great part of the booty carried to Rome after the conquest of Macedon and they may even have been absorbed into the currency of the Republic. They also travelled north and west, perhaps via Rome, to be imitated by the Gauls and the Britons, in whose hands the classical forms of Apollo's profile and Philip's chariot disintegrated into particles of Celtic ornament [figure 32].

The westward spread of Greek coinage was gradual and fortuitous. Its redevelopment in the east was sudden, deliberately fostered by the policy of Alexander. Since the Athenian coinage was the most widely accepted currency in the west, Alexander abandoned his father's clumsy dual system and adopted the Attic standard for silver as for gold. The new types which Alexander took for his silver were also well fitted to their eventual role as designs for an imperial coinage: not only had Heracles and Zeus an obvious panhellenic significance, but Heracles could be identified with Melqart, his Phoenician counterpart whose oldest temple was at Tyre, and the figure of Zeus on the reverse was iconographically almost indistinguishable from Baal as he appeared on coins of Tarsus in Cilicia. Most of the independent Greek coinages, except those most firmly established like the Athenian, were swamped by the great and uniform coinage of Alexander, which was supplied not only from the Macedonian mines but from the captured treasuries of the Great King and was issued from twenty principal mints in the various provinces of the Empire.

33 Syracuse, silver tetradrachm, c. 410 BC, signed by Euainetos [twice actual size].

17

34 Pontus, silver tetradrachm, *c.* 200 BC, Mithradates III; a notable example of Hellenistic coin portraiture [actual size].

After the death of Darius in 330 BC Alexander had taken the title of *basileus*, and on some coins of Alexandria, where he was regarded as a god in the tradition of the Pharaohs, the face of Heracles seems to have assumed his likness. To appear on the coinage had hitherto been the preserve of the gods. After his death Alexander was the first mortal to break this monopoly, but he did so equivocally by becoming in a sense a god himself. This can be seen in Egypt on coins issued by Ptolemy Soter [figure 29], and, more surprisingly, in Ionia, where one of his generals, Lysimachus, king of Thrace, issued coins with a fine portrait of his master wearing the ram's horn of Ammon [figure 19]. The principle was soon extended to include the living, first by Ptolemy Soter [figure 21], whose inheritance of Alexander's Egyptian kingdom entitled him to divine honours, and a little later by Seleucus, who had held the satrapy of Babylon and ruled the central part of Alexander's Empire. To the Greeks, however, this idea was presumptuous. In Pergamum, ruled by the family of one of Lysimachus' lieutenants, the tradition of posthumous portraits was maintained, and for years the coinage carried the likeness of the dynasty's founder, the eunuch Philetaerus [figure 19]. Not until 200 BC did a king of Macedon, Philip V, first venture to issue a portrait coinage, and he was also one of the last, because his son Perseus was conquered by the Romans in 168 BC [figure 11].

In Egypt the royal portrait was in a sense divine and remained fixed for generations; but the Seleucids claimed no divinity and each king in turn set his own portrait on the coinage [figure 11]. The Greek artist's love of truth rose above even the temptation to flatter a powerful autocrat, and these portrait coins are remarkable for their faithful record of the strength or weakness of the successive kings. The tradition was taken up on the borders of the Seleucid kingdom, in Pontus on the Black Sea and in Bactria, the furthermost of Alexander's satrapies, which became independent in 250 BC. Perhaps the finest coin-portrait of all is one of Mithradates III of Pontus in about 200 BC, a touching study of the middle-aged man which epitomizes the cares of kingship [figure 34]. Some of the Bactrians, such as Antimachus [figure 11] are unknown except by their coins, but the series of portraits which survives tells more of the character of these vigorous frontier kings than is known of many better documented rulers; nor perhaps is it fanciful to see the upstart pride of the rebel in the great gold piece of Eucratides, *basileus megalos* (maharajah), minted in 160 BC [figure 1].

There is some degeneracy in the later Hellenistic coinage, and by 100 BC Mithradates the Great of Pontus had abandoned the formal restraint of his predecessors for a full-blown romanticism. Subject, however, to the invigorating discipline of Rome, Greek engravers were to work on in a new idiom.

ROMANS AND BYZANTINES

35 Roman Empire, as, *c.* AD 22–30, Tiberius; a portrait of the deified Augustus [enlarged 3 : 1].

THE FIRST ROMAN COINAGE was in bronze, the natural metallic currency of Italy. The cities of Sicily and Magna Graecia had been among the earliest of all Greek mints to issue bronze coins in the fifth century BC, and the original silver coinage of both the Sicilians and the Etruscans [figure 37] was based on a bronze weight standard, the *litra,* which was equivalent to a small silver coin worth about one-fifth of an Attic drachma. However, Roman civilization was far behind that of Sicily or Etruria and the Romans do not seem to have felt any need for coined money until the third century BC. The formal conveyancing contract of

36 Roman Republic, silver denarius, *c.* 45 BC, moneyer T. Carisius, showing obverse the head of Juno Moneta, in whose temple the mint was situated, and reverse the traditional emblems of the moneyer [actual size].

37 Populonia, silver stater, *c.* 350 BC; the Etruscan silver coinage was originally based on a bronze weight standard [twice actual size].

mancipatio, which dates from before the Law of the Twelve Tables (450 BC), calls for bronze money and a pair of scales, but the law required the buyer under the contract to strike the scales with the bronze, a procedure which suggests an uncoined lump of some size. The first Roman money to have any sort of identifying mark, the so-called *aes signatum* [figure 41], which was probably minted soon after 300 BC, would have served this purpose well. The representation of an ox on the earliest of these cast ingots was apposite, as the word *pecunia,* money, was derived from *pecus,* cattle.

About 289 BC the Senate, according to tradition, established a board of three junior magistrates to be responsible for the issue of coinage. They were known as the *tresviri aere argento auro flando feriundo (III viri aaaff),* the three men for casting and striking bronze, silver and gold. Their office, which ranked below that of quaestor, was a first step in the *cursus honorum,* and after 140 BC, when the president of the board habitually signed the coins in full, the names of several future consuls appeared among them. When other magistrates, such as a quaestor or the curule aedile, issued coins, as they sometimes did, it was usually by special authority of the Senate and they acknowledged this by adding SC *(Senatus Consulto)* after their signatures. The mint was under the patronage of Juno Moneta (the Adviser) and it was probably situated in her temple. Her head appears on some late republican coins [figure 36], and her name is the very origin of the word 'money'.

At about the time of the institution of the *III viri aaaff* there appeared the first Roman pieces which, being round and roughly adjusted in weight, are clearly recognizable as coins. They are known as *aes grave* and, like the *aes signatum,* they were cast, not struck. They carried a mark of value and each denomination had a distinctive design. It is characteristic of the Romans that their earliest coinage should have been so methodical and so ponderous. Their types also were essentially Latin [figure 52]: on the *as,* which was the unit of account, was Janus the ancient god-king of Latium, while the prow had been an emotive symbol to the Romans at least since 338 BC, when they had made their public-speaking platform out of the captured *rostra* of the ships of Antium.

The *aes grave* was an inconvenient trading currency, and, although bronze in a modified from continued as an important part of the domestic coinage, it was not long before Rome came into line with the other city states of the Mediterranean and issued struck silver coins. Pliny the Elder declares in his Natural History that the Romans first issued silver in 269 BC, and that these coins were *denarii,* but modern scholarship has found difficulty in reconciling the two parts of this statement. The date of the first denarius, originally a silver coin worth 10 bronze

38 Memorial relief (c. 15 BC) to P. Licinius Stolo, formerly one of the *tresviri aaaff*, erected by two of his Greek freedmen, P. Licinius Philonicus *(left)*, who was a lictor, and his father P. Licinius Demetrius, a die-cutter. In the pediment are the emblems of a moneyer: dies, hammer and tongs; in the left plinth the lictor's fasces; in the right the graving-tool, awl, knife, and bowdrill, the tools of a die-engraver.

asses, is still in dispute. The most generally received theory brings the date down to the Second Punic War (218–201), and ascribes to 269 BC and the First Punic War a series of didrachms, with attendant smaller silver and bronze, which read variously ROMANO [rum] and ROMA.

Some of the types of the early silver were Roman in their associations: Janus [figure 43], the wolf and the twins, and later, on the first denarii, the war goddess Bellona and Castor and Pollux. However, the style of these coins, unlike that of the *aes grave*, was Hellenistic. The strength of Hellenistic art was in its portraiture. Its interpretation of mythological or allegorical subjects was generally weak, and the early Roman silver shows

21

39 Roman Republic, bronze sestertius, c. 38 BC, struck in Gaul; Octavian (reverse) boasts his special relationship with Julius Caesar (obverse) [actual size].

it at its most feeble. We cannot really believe in the horse-power of the chariots which race across these coins. They are like the Victor Emmanuel memorial in modern Rome, an empty rhetorical statement of an idea played out long before. What the Romans really cared about were their homes, their families and their ancestors, but they were at first inhibited by republican sentiment from introducing such personal themes into a public matter. The Roman coinage became lively only after this prejudice had given way in the first century BC.

The coinage of the second century was artistically uneventful, but economically and politically it was of central importance in the controversy between the rival parties in Rome. The Senate financed the public debt by deliberately reducing the value of

40 Roman Empire, sestertius, Nero (AD 54-68); imperial coin portraiture reached its height under Nero, who struck this coin to commemorate the closing of the temple of Janus in AD 66 [enlarged 3:1].

41 Roman Republic, so-called *aes signatum, c.* 300 BC; pieces of cast bronze like this are the earliest identifiable Roman money. The Latin word *pecunia* (money) was derived from *pecus* (cattle) [actual size].

the currency. The weight of the denarius fell gradually until 155 BC, and from time to time a proportion of plated coin was included in the silver issues. The bronze was first transformed into a fiduciary coinage at a fraction of its original weight; then, because it was impossible to re-establish it on a valid basis secure against manipulation, it was suspended. The policy of debasement was opposed by the moneyed non-senatorial class of *equites* who relied upon a sound currency for their trading operations. Their opposition to the Senate went through several fluctuations of fortune, but when finally Sulla, the senatorial general, assumed control of the Republic in 88 BC, debased coinage continued in full spate, and a praetor, M. Marius Gratidianus, who had invented a process for telling good money from bad, was murdered in one of the dictator's proscriptions.

The coin-types in the last century of the Republic compounded religious and family feeling with political allusion. Once the traditional types, such as Bellona and the Dioscuri, were discarded, it was natural for a moneyer to choose as his type a god with which his own family had a special association and, if the reverse type was to allude to the legendary history of Rome, to take an episode in which his own ancestors had been involved. Enough of republican spirit remained at first rigorously to exclude portraits of the living, but the Romans accorded a sort of domestic divinity to their own ancestors, whose death-masks the family religiously preserved, and it therefore required no great leap sometimes to replace the familiar god by the famous

23

42 Roman Republic, silver denarius, c. 96–94 BC, moneyer P. Cornelius Lentulus; obverse Hercules, reverse triumphal investiture.

43 Roman Republic, silver didrachm, after 269 BC; the earliest Roman silver coins were Hellenistic in style and conformed to Greek weight standards [actual size].

44 Roman Republic, silver denarius, c. 65 BC, moneyer Q. Pomponius Rufus: obverse the moneyer's ancestor; reverse Sulla, who died in 78 BC [actual size].

45 Roman Republic, silver denarius, c. 42-38 BC; issued by Sextus Pompey in Sicily; the portrait is of his father, Pompey the Great [actual size].

46 Roman Republic, gold aureus, c. 46 BC, moneyer A. Hirtius, obverse portrait of Julius Caesar [actual size].

47 Roman Republic, silver denarius, c. 43 BC, moneyer L. Plaetorius Cestianus; a boast of the Ides of March, struck for M. Junius Brutus in the East [actual size].

48 Roman Republic, gold aureus, c. 41 BC, moneyer M. Barbatius, quaestor; a coin of the Seond Triumvirate, obverse Mark Antony, reverse Octavian [actual size].

49 Roman Empire, silver denarius, Tiberius (AD 14–37). 'Whose is this image and superscription?' This was the common coin of the Empire in the time of Christ [actual size].

50 Roman Empire, gold aureus, Claudius (AD 41-54); here Claudius appears with his stepson Nero [actual size].

51　The only known ancient representation of a coining scene: a fourth-century memorial showing two moneyers at work.

52 Roman Republic, bronze as, so-called *aes grave*, c. 289 BC; and early cast coin with a mark of value and the types of Janus and the prow [actual size].

ancestor. This was not just antiquarianism. The Romans considered history primarily as having a profound moral significance for the present, and they drew on the ancient symbolism of the death-mask and the temple to express their hopes and fears about their own times. Thus on a coin of P. Cornelius Lentulus (*c.* 98 BC), Hercules, associated on the reverse with a triumphal investiture, represents the victorious return of Marius from the Cimbrian war [figure 42]. Concordia on a denarius of P. Fonteius Capito (*c.* 61 BC) is a hopeful invocation in the factious years that led up to the First Triumvirate. A posthumous portrait of Sulla on a coin of Q. Pomponius Rufus is a clear statement of political loyalty [figure 44], while Julius Caesar might have seen a warning in coins of M. Junius Brutus struck in about 50 BC, with the bust of Liberty on one side and on the other Brutus the First Consul, who expelled the Tarquins.

The propagandist content of the republican coinage was not blatant, although it was well understood by a rhetorical and politically conscious people such as the Romans. However, in the last year of Julius Caesar's dictatorship there was a change to the overt cult of personality. On coins struck in Rome he placed not only his name and titles, but also his portrait; only a veil which, on most of them, covered his head as if for some priestly function, made any concession to republican decency [figure 46].

It came to be an established convention of the Republic that a general's *imperium* included a power to issue coins for his soldiers on a campaign. During the civil wars the several protagonists made full use of this power and of the opportunity which it gave them to advertise themselves. Naturally the triumvirs followed Caesar's precedent in the matter of coin portraiture with least inhibition and they appeared separately or together on a large number of issues [figure 48]. However the dictator's enemies were not slow to follow. In Sicily, Sextus Pompey struck a few coins with his own portrait, though he found perhaps that his great father's likeness appealed more to his soldiers' loyalty [figure 45]. Brutus, with cynical disregard for true republican feeling, issued denarii with his portrait on one side and the daggers of the Ides of March on the other [figure 47]. Only the coinage of C. Cassius in Asia was scrupulously traditional.

Among the coins of the triumvirs, those of Octavian stand out from the others. Squarely basing his claim to rule on his adoption by Julius Caesar, he made less use than either Antony or Lepidus of the title which they all shared, often styling himself simply *Caesar Divi F.,* Caesar the son of a god (literally: of one who has become a god), and instead of a portrait of one of his colleagues, joined that of the late dictator with his own [figure 39]. He never used on a coin the name Octavian which he derived from his original family. He took the title of Augustus in 27 BC.

53 Roman Empire, sestertius, AD 141-61, Antoninus Pius; the great number of coins issued by Antoninus Pius in honour of his dead wife, Faustina the Elder, was perhaps a measure of the bereaved emperor's personal sorrow [enlarged 3:1].

The great achievement of Augustus was his tactful redirection of republican institutions to new and grander purposes. The coinage, which he found in a chaotic state and left fit to serve the requirements of a great empire, has, however, a special significance. Augustus drew the moral from the propagandist issues of the previous seventy years, and made it into a delicate instrument for public relations. The coinage of imperial Rome, as he created it, has therefore a double interest. It illustrates not only the monetary system of nearly the whole civilized world during three centuries, but also much of general policy.

54 Roman Empire, brass sestertius, Titus (AD 79–81), reverse, commemorating the building of the Colosseum [actual size].

55 Roman Empire, brass dupondius, *c*. 20 BC, Augustus, moneyer T. Crispinus; a typically political coin of the first part of Augustus' reign with references to *Tribunicia Potestas* (obverse) and *S(enatus) C(onsulto)* (reverse) [actual size].

56 Roman Empire, copper as, Caligula (AD 37–41); reverse Vesta, meant to be identified with Augustus' wife, Livia [actual size].

Augustus regarded it as of first importance to keep the coinage of precious metals in his own hands in order to control the pay of the legions, on which his power was based; and his distribution of mints appears to have been founded partly on political and partly on strategic considerations. In the west, the discovery of dies in various parts of Gaul and Spain proves that the minting of precious metals, which were mostly mined in Spain, was decentralized. However Lugdunum in Gaul appears eventually to have become the only administrative centre, in preference to Rome itself, where Augustus could not with discretion infringe the Senate's constitutional right to mint, since he was theoretically the restorer of the Republic. In the east, most of the major mints, such as those at Antioch and Ephesus, continued to operate under imperial authority, striking not only denarii and gold but also tetradrachms of various Greek standards, most of which were tariffed under the imperial system at three denarii. In Egypt, always the emperor's peculiar province, Augustus and his successors continued in their own names the issue of base silver tetradrachms like those of the later Ptolemies; these were tariffed at one denarius. Nowhere was independent coinage in precious metals permitted, although some former city states were allowed a bronze coinage of their own as a concession to their ancient traditions of minting. By a stroke of luck for the Romans, the exhaustion of the mines at Laurium brought to a natural end the Athenian silver coinage, which it might have been deemed sacrilegious to suppress.

The Senate's claims, if such they can be called, to have some part in the currency of the Roman Empire, were met by the arrangements which Augustus made for the base metal coinage. The failure of the republican bronze coinage had caused inconvenience, but there was still some danger that it would be unpopular if it were reintroduced. Augustus therefore introduced coinage in new metals, brass (with which Julius Caesar also had experimented) and pure copper. In fact brass was cheaper than bronze, but it looked more expensive. As the emperor monopolized the supply of zinc from Spain, he could fix the price at which it came on the market and give the higher denominations, the *sestertius* and the *dupondius*, an artificial worth equal to their current value of one-quarter and one-eighth of a denarius. The lower denominations, the as and its fractions, in pure copper, were accepted for their very full weight and attractive appearance. It would be wrong to suggest that the Senate actually controlled this coinage, since Augustus controlled the Senate by virtue of his *auctoritas* and the *tribunicia potestas*. It was, however, administered through the Senate and the senatorial mint in Rome, and the coins bore the mark of the constitutional process through which they were issued: either *CA* for *Caesaris Auctoritate* in the east, or, in the west, *SC* for

57 Roman Empire, gold aureus, c. 160, Antoninus Pius; a portrait of his daughter-in-law, Faustina the Younger, the wife of Marcus Aurelius [enlarged $1\frac{1}{3}$: 1].

58 *(left)* Roman Empire, gold aureus, Diocletian (284–305), mint of Carthage and *(right)* bronze follis, Maximian (286–305); the physical difference between the two colleagues is here minimized by the similarity of treatment [actual size].

59 Roman Empire, gold solidus, Contantine the Great (307–37); with Constantine and his sons (figure 67) the style of portraiture becomes uncompromisingly hieratic [enlarged 3 : 1].

Senatus Consulto, the decree of the Senate which it had no option but to pass [figure 55]. *SC* became the regular formula for the *aes* coinage and survived until the third century, long after any pretence of senatorial interest in the mint had been abandoned.

If ever a dictator were to assume control of the United States, he would use all the resources of press, radio and television to put across the idea that there was nothing un-American about his activities. This was exactly the position of Augustus and his successors, and they used the coinage, which was the best means of public communication at their disposal, to display the essentially Roman character of the régime. They appealed directly to the Romans' feeling for history by the use of republican symbols such as the civic crown of oak leaves [figure 55] and later by a succession of anniversary and commemorative issues, and to their family pride by the apotheosis of the imperial ancestors. Since the emperor himself was *Pater Patriae,* his own family was in a sense related to the Roman people and his ancestors became as it were by adoption the household gods of the State. Julius Caesar and Augustus were both formally deified [figure 35], but the shadowy position of Augustus' wife Livia, who appeared on a number of coins implicitly identified with Vesta, the goddess of hearth and home [figure 56], reflects perhaps more truly the allusive way in which the Romans at first approached this idea of deification. Caligula, in a pious phase, issued coins in the names of no less than seven dead relations, and later Claudius introduced portraits of living imperial ladies and children [figure 50]. The formal deification of deceased members of the imperial family reached a climax under the adoptive emperors in the second century AD when Antoninus Pius issued an enormous coinage in the name of his dead wife Faustina the Elder [figure 53], but it fell into disuse in the face of the monotheistic beliefs fashionable in the latter part of the third century. Nevertheless the honouring of the imperial family on the coinage, which incidentally says much for the status of Roman women, continued well into the Byzantine period.

The cult of the imperial family depended for much of its success upon the quality of portraiture, and in this the emperors were well served. The death-mask tradition of the Republic combined with the academic skill of the Hellenistic artists to produce the series of portraits from Claudius to Caracalla which are the glory of Roman coinage. Set in a framework of beautifully proportioned lettering, these portraits have an ordered restraint which is typically Roman. They were copied from official *imagines* which were circulated to the various mints from Rome. It is remarkable that the character of a Nero should come so strongly through a filter of that kind [figure 40].

The reverses of imperial coins were given over to detailed information, both true and false, about the régime, and to ex-

29

hortation. Concrete achievements, like the completion of public buildings or monuments [figure 54], were a matter for straightforward illustration, but most of the ideas were more complex. Concepts such as the capture of a province, the morale of the legions or the maintenance of the corn supply, together with all the possible virtues of the emperor, his courage, piety or foresight, were conveyed by means of personifications, whose curious symbolism of gesture and attribute, so artificial to our eyes, was readily understood by the ordinary citizen and had an important place in Roman religious thinking.

The flow of information on Roman coins is a useful source of pro-government evidence to set against the sometimes hostile testimony of historians. Clemency is not a virtue which we readily associate with Tiberius, but if a coin of his draws attention to it, it is to be taken seriously as being either true, or at least something which Tiberius wanted the Romans to believe. If the frequent references to Nero's public works draw the taunt that

60 A late Roman bas-relief from Noviomagus in eastern Gaul showing payment of taxes. Tax requirements played an increasingly important part in the operations of the mints in the later days of the Empire.

61 Byzantine Empire, solidi, Justinian II (second reign, 705–11) reverse, another coin obverse, and Anastasius II (713–16) reverse; the first coin shows the facing head of Christ and the second the emperor with his son Tiberius; Anastasius' reversion to the cross, instead of the head of Christ, is perhaps a sign of iconoclast influence [twice actual size].

Mussolini made the trains run on time, we must at least take note of his claim to have established world peace, which seems to be implied in the type of *Securitas Augusti*. The Romans may have looked back regretfully a few years later when Otho, at the height of the civil war of 69, recalled this type with his own *Securitas P(opuli) R(omani)*. This must have been pure wishful thinking, an appeal by the most Neronian of the four emperors of that year for a return to the good old days. The conquest of Britain by Claudius, and of Judaea by Vespasian, are commemorated on coins of those emperors [figure 62]. Trajan's coinage, like his column, is a continuous record of military conquest, while Hadrian's sets out in detail his liberal policy of provincial settlement and his visits to every part of the Empire [figure 64].

A large part of the heavy financial burden of the administration and defence of the Roman Empire was carried by revenue

31

62 Roman Empire, silver denarius, Vespasian (69-79); the reverse commemorates the final conquest of the Jews by his son Titus [enlarged 3 : 1].

from the coinage, which was gradually reduced in weight and debased. To avoid cutting its own throat, the government in the third century insisted on payment of taxes in bullion. By the time of Caracalla the denarius was only 40 per cent silver, and after that emperor's introduction of a new coin one and a half times the weight of the denarius, but probably tariffed at two, the situation grew out of control. During the sole reign of Gallienus (259–68), the intrinsic worth of the 'silver' coin dropped to almost nothing and, as the government's credit was gone, it was valueless. Great hoards of the debased coins of Gallienus have been found, mute evidence of a financial collapse as disastrous as that of Germany in 1923. The Empire's debt was finally paid by its ruined citizens.

The bankruptcy of the old Roman Empire was only one aspect of its total collapse. Its revival under the succession of great soldiers and administrators, Aurelian, Diocletian and Constantine, also led to its complete transformation, and this is reflected in its coinage, which underwent a series of reforms under those three emperors and re-emerged utterly changed in appearance, in content and in organization.

The most obvious change was in the appearance of the emperor himself. With the eastward shift of the political centre of gravity, the emperors, who since the reign of Septimius Severus (193–211) had shown less disposition to uphold even the forms of the principate, became more autocratic and remote from their subjects, like other oriental despots. This led to greater stylization of portraiture as the importance of the ruler's personality declined in relation to his office. It is already quite hard to distinguish at first glance between the portraits of Diocletian and Maximian [figure 58], despite Maximian's coarse features and snub nose. The appearance of Constantine and his sons, diademed and in one instance haloed, is uncompromisingly hieratic [figures 59 and 67]; and with the first Byzantine emperors nearly all semblance of portraiture disappears, until it is revived in a new form in the reign of Heraclius. The frequent appearance of military dress in coin-portraits and the adoption of more fulsome titles, *Dominus Noster* and even *Beatissimus*, are two other signs of a changed attitude.

The currency reforms of Diocletian and Constantine have not yet been fully elucidated, but the corner-stone of each was a gold coin of guaranteed weight and fineness. That is the significance of the name *solidus* which was given to Constantine's coin, struck at the rate of seventy-two to the Roman pound. Silver coin was issued only rarely, but then it was very pure. Thus far, the reforms were beneficial, but the system was fatally defective. The bulk of the currency was in silvered bronze, tariffed by the government at a value well above its true worth. The over-valuation would not have mattered if it had been con-

63   Roman Empire, brass sestertius, Antoninus Pius (138-61); the figure of Britannia on the reverse was copied for the copper of Charles II of England, and still continues on the English penny [actual size].

64   Roman Empire, brass sestertius, Hadrian (117-38); a commentary on the emperor's enlightened policy towards the provinces: the reverse legend, ADVENTUS HISPANIAE, commemorates his visit to his native Spain [actual size].

65   Byzantine Empire; bronze 40 nummia, 538–39, Justinian I; the 'M' on the reverse is the mark of value, and the 'B' underneath is the mark of the workshop in the mint of Constantinople [actual size].

66 Byzantine Empire, gold solidus, John Zimisces (969–76); the Virgin crowning the emperor, a typical example of tenth-century inconography [twice actual size].

vertible into solidi at a fixed rate, but it was not. Only the solidus was accepted in payment of taxes and it was traded in the market as bullion. The over-valued bronze, the *follis* and other denominations, carried the whole burden of daily internal commercial transactions and, despite edicts to control prices, there was continuing inflation as the market rating of these coins sank to its proper level.

The high degree of civil organization of the Empire from the time of Diocletian appears both in the uniformity of the coinage and in the system of mint marks. All provincial and local issues ceased, and almost every diocese, as the territorial divisions were called, was provided with its own mint. Coins were usually marked with the name or initial of the mint and, a little later, with the code number of the *officina*, or workshop, also.

In the western half of the Empire the mints fell one by one into barbarian hands and the system of bronze coinage broke down completely. In the east the consolidation of the Byzantine Empire was marked by a coinage reform under Anastasius (491–518), which once again re-established a bronze coinage, characterized by its good weight and clear marks of value [figure 65]. Bronze coinage, however, came and went, and silver coin continued to be rare: the timeless quality of Byzantium was reflected in the solidus, which, true to its name, was maintained in weight and fineness until the eleventh century. Internally it kept its original function as a coin for the payment of taxes, but it was used also for external payments and subsidies and a coin of such prestige was bound to play an important part in international trade. From the ninth century, the *bezant*, as it was called in the west, was virtually the only gold coin of Christendom, and found a place in the treasuries, if not in the fairs and markets, of mediaeval Europe.

The Byzantine coinage in gold, silver and bronze reflects suprisingly little of the great periods of Byzantine art in the sixth and eleventh centuries. In the time of Justinian, the types

68 Byzantine Empire, silver milaresion, Leo V (813-20); the lasting influence of the iconoclasts is visible in the austere calligraphic style of Byzantine silver [actual size].

were still fixed, as they had been in the late Roman period, with the emperor's helmeted bust full-face [figure 65], or, as on the *triens* (one-third of a solidus), his diademed profile, neither of which had even the merit of being well drawn. By the time of the second period under Alexius Comnenus (1081-1118), the coinage was already beginning to show signs of economic degeneration, which has usually been discouraging to artists. The coins of finest style were struck between these two periods, beginning in the reign of Heraclius (610–41) [figure 69], when Byzantine die-engravers seem first to have found their idiom, which was one of sensitive observation disciplined by extreme formality of composition, and ending soon after Michael IV (1034–41) began to tamper with the purity of the solidus.

The iconoclast controversy was, until the Fourth Crusade, perhaps the most deeply felt experience in Byzantine history, and both sides left their mark on the coinage. The image of Christ was introduced on the reverse of the solidus in the first reign of Justinian II (685–95) [figure 61], and on some coins it was, it seems, even intended to supplant the emperor as the principal figure. It was suppressed in 717 by Leo III, founder of the iconoclastic Isaurian dynasty. For a period, even secular portraits were formalized and the facing busts of the emperors were deliberately drained of all personality, their features treated as pure pattern. The silver, on which no representation of the emperor appeared, became even more austere, its whole design an abstraction of lettering and symbols [figure 68]. But the precedent of Justinian II was not forgotten, and after the restoration of the icons in 843, the Pantocrator was adopted as a regular type on both gold and bronze, while the Virgin was represented on gold after the time of Leo VI (886–912), who was especially devoted to her cult [figure 66].

The Byzantine coinage was conservative, but not unchanging. As a minor battleground between Greek and Latin in its inscriptions and between iconoclast and iconodule in its imagery, it gives a fair picture of that remote and contentious civilization.

69 Byzantine Empire, gold solidus, Heraclius (610–41), mint of Constantinople; the emperor is shown with his son Heraclius Constantine [twice actual size].

35

EUROPEAN COINAGE IN THE MIDDLE AGES

71 Rome, bronze, Theodahad, king of the Ostrogoths (534-6); realistic portrait in the Roman style, but of a barbarian king [actual size].

72 Visigothic Spain, gold triens, Svinthila (621-31), mint of Merida; the style of Visigothic coins was barbarous but not degenerate. Their system of mints was highly organized [actual size].

70 (opposite) A capital from the abbey of St Georges de Boscherville in Normandy (eleventh century), showing a moneyer at work; the lower die is set into the anvil by his knee.

THE BARBARIANS WHO OVERRAN the western half of the Empire in the fifth century had no coinage of their own: either they took over what they found or they let it lapse altogether, as in Britain for about two hundred years. In some places the invaders maintained the Roman mints as they did other imperial institutions, and their kings, who in a few cases claimed to represent the imperial power without aspiring to its full titles and privileges, issued coins in the name of the only emperor they knew, the one at Constantinople. Some of these coins were distinguished by the insertion of the initial or monogram of a king or of the place where they were struck.

While the gold solidus remained the standard coin of the Byzantine Empire, in the poorer west the triens to a great extent supplanted it. Silver was rare, as it had been under the later emperors, and for common use there was only bronze. This was less exclusively an imperial preserve: the sons of Clovis, Theodoric of Austrasia (511–34) and Childebert of Paris (511–58), both issued bronze coins in their own names; and Theodahad the Ostrogoth (534–36) introduced a remarkable but short-lived coinage displaying not only his name but his portrait [figure 71]. Artistically the bronze of this period was usually poor, but at Rome Theodahad employed at least one die-engraver who had the Roman gift for realistic portraiture and the imagination to adapt it to the informal magnificence of a barbarian king. The coins of the first king to break the imperial monopoly in gold, Theodebert of Austrasia (534–48), were artistically less enterprising: the legend DN Theodebertus Victor proclaimed the Frank's independence and his victory over Justinian's army in Italy, but the facing portrait was still unquestionably that of a Byzantine emperor [figure 75].

In the west, bronze coinage and the rare issues of silver both came to an end in the middle of the sixth century. For the next hundred years the only issues were of gold, a strange situation for a poor economy, but the gold was used for fiscal purposes and royal gifts and subsidies, while for everyday use there was no new coinage at all. Among the most prolific gold coinages of the time was that of the Visigoths in Spain and Narbonnese Gaul. This was regularly issued by all but one of the twenty short-lived kings who reigned from 568 until the extinction of the Visigothic kingdom by the Moors in 711. There was one coin only, the triens, but, broader and thinner than before, it

37

73 *(left to right)* Fritzlar, bracteate, Abbot Siegfried III von Eppstein (1230–49); Erfurt, bracteate, Henry I von Haarburg, Archbishop of Mainz (1142–53); Brandenburg, bracteate, Margrave Otto I (1170–84). The bracteates of eastern Germany are the only mediaeval coins which worthily reflect the style of Romanesque art [enlarged $1\frac{1}{2}$: 1].

74 Frankish Empire, silver denier, Charlemagne (768–814), mint of Milan [actual size].

had almost the diameter of a solidus. Each coin was issued bearing the name of the king and of one of about eighty mints from Narbonne to Oporto. The style, though barbarous, was by no means degenerate. The original Roman designs were broken up, but not into disorder and the forms abstracted from them were well defined and well balanced [figure 72].

The regularity of the Visigothic coinage suggests a high degree of civil organization. In France the weakness of the Merovingians became apparent in the usurpation of their minting rights by their subjects. When in the middle of the seventh century the Franks began to coin again in silver, only one of the new denarii was issued in the name of the king, Caribert II (629–31). It seems possible that for a brief period before the extinction of the gold coinage at the end of the seventh century, there was a scale of value by which one pound weight of silver was equal to twenty solidi (a name which by then had perhaps been transferred to gold trientes) and 240 of these denarii. It is a paradox of economic history that the system of £.s.d. may have been conceived at this obscure point of transition when economic activity in Europe was at its lowest.

The Merovingian denarii were soon imitated by the Anglo-Saxons and the Frisians, between whom there was an active trade across the North Sea. These pieces were issued in large numbers; most were copies of late Roman coins, degenerate in

75 Austrasia, gold solidus, Theodebert (534–48), the first coin in the name of a Frankish king; though the name is that of Theodebert, the face is still that of a Byzantine emperor [actual size].

76 *(top row)* Mercia, pennies, Offa (757–96), struck at Canterbury (the third coin reverse). *(bottom row)* Mercia, penny, Coenwulf (796–822), London; Kent, penny, Cuthred (801?–7), Canterbury; Frankish Empire, denier, Louis the Pious (814–40). The Canterbury pennies of Offa are the most remarkable artistic achievement in the early mediaeval coinage [enlarged $1\frac{1}{2}:1$].

style, and were issued anonymously, but late in the seventh century some issues appeared in the names of kings of Northumbria. The northern kingdom maintained this coinage until the Danish conquest in the ninth century; by then it was debased to copper and played no further part in international trade.

It now seems that the monetary reforms of the first Carolingians were less sweeping than was once supposed, and that there was little difference in weight between a Merovingian denarius and a denier of Pepin the Short. Nevertheless, the changes at this time were psychologically important. The new coins were struck in the king's name, showing that royal control over the currency was re-established. They were made broader and thinner after the manner of Visigothic and Moorish coins, the blanks being cut out from hammered sheets of metal before striking; which suggests, in so far as this made the coins easier to handle, that there was a change in emphasis from money used as a store of wealth to money as a means of daily exchange. Finally, the exploitation of silver mines at Melle in Poitou brought in a new supply of metal: the very quantity of Carolingian coinage makes it different from the Merovingian issues.

In the eighth century most of the population lived within a manorial economy in which rights and obligations were ex-

77 Rome, silver denier, Pope Stephen VI and Charles the Fat (885-91); the Pope's monogram is on one side, the emperor's name on the other [actual size].

78 Frankish empire, silver denier, Louis the Pious (814-40), reverse; the Roman basilica on this common coin was to last on the French coinage through various evolutions until the fourteenth century [actual size].

79 Poitou, silver denier, twelfth century; the name on the coin is still that of the ninth-century Charles the Bald, but this piece may have been issued by Richard Coeur de Lion, c. 1170 [actual size].

pressed in kind: there was no need for a valuable or sophisticated coinage, because it was required mainly for external transactions and by the minority who lived by trade. The Carolingian coinage, therefore, consisting only of silver in a single small denomination, was not a great commercial medium, but it suited the needs of the time and would probably have spread rapidly even without Charlemagne's conquests in Germany and Italy [figure 74]. Within twenty-five years of Pepin's reform, two minor kings of Kent, Heahbert and Ecgbert, issued pennies like Charlemagne's deniers, and Offa, king of Mercia, after he conquered Kent in 783–4, developed a substantial penny coinage.

By the end of the eighth century the penny coinage was established all over western Europe from the Tiber to the Thames: in Rome itself the Pope and the emperor issued denarii conjointly with the emperor's name on one side and the Pope's monogram on the other [figure 77]. The coins of Charlemagne and his immediate successors were neatly made, but the regular types were rather dull: a cross, the imperial monogram, a Roman basilica or the mint name in straight lines across the field [figures 74 and 78]. The chief interest of these motifs lies in their continued use over many centuries, and in their evolution after their original significance was forgotten [figure 91]. The emperor's portrait was rarely used [figure 76].

If, as is now the case with some Bactrian kings, Offa and Charlemagne come to survive only in the evidence of their coins, Offa will at last achieve the pre-eminence which he vainly sought during his lifetime. His Canterbury pennies are in the best traditions of English art, imaginative and varied in conception and exquisitely worked in detail. His successors never achieved anything as good, though there is a certain rustic charm about a London coin of Coenwulf, king of Mercia, and a few pennies of Cuthred, king of Kent, have some of the neatness of Offa's [figure 76].

The contrast between the penny coinages of England and Europe is not only an artistic one. From the time of Offa, the English kings kept strict control over minting arrangements. In the tenth century, when West Saxon over-lordship was extended over all of England except the Viking areas of the north, the whole kingdom received a uniform coinage, distributed from a large number of local mints, to which the dies were supplied by a few central or regional authorities. The Anglo-Saxon system, which was elaborated by King Eadgar (959–75), seems to have worked very efficiently. It bore without apparent strain not only the enormous issues of Aethelred II for the payment of Danegeld, but also the changes in type, involving the recoinage of most of the money in circulation, which Aethelred and his successors periodically ordained as a source of revenue. Foreign coin was kept out of the country, so that internally the national coinage

80 England, silver penny, William I (1066-87), moneyer Colswegen of Hastings; this belongs to the first of William's issues. There was little change of personnel at the mint: Colswegen appears on coins of Edward the Confessor and Harold [actual size].

81 England, silver penny, Edward the Confessor (1042-66), moneyer Godwin of Chichester; the design of the seated king was one of the most ambitious of the Anglo-Saxon series. The birds on the reverse were, in the thirteenth century, interpreted as the Confessor's coat of arms [actual size].

could hold its value by royal decree, regardless of its frequent changes of weight. This last arrangement was the only one which William I [figure 80] discontinued after the Conquest. The Norman coinage was the worst in France, and he was pleased to maintain in his new realm a system which was both efficient and profitable; but by fixing the weight of the currency, he made it more acceptable abroad, where henceforth it was known by the new name of sterling.

The regular change of types continued for nearly a century after the Conquest, and only in the reign of Stephen was there any lapse of exclusive royal control [figure 85]. Henry II, however, realized that the sterling's reputation for stability was not improved by constant changes in its appearance. He reversed the earlier policy, and from 1158 until 1489 the type of the silver was changed only three times.

The Carolingian coinage was originally administered for the king by his counts. In the mid-ninth century the kings began the practice of conferring the right of minting on great ecclesiastics and, as the royal power declined, the counts took the full responsibility and profit of minting upon themselves. The earliest of these issues were struck in the name of the king with no acknowledgment of their feudal origin, but early in the tenth century some counts joined their own name with the king's or even left the latter out. Few of the great feudatories resisted the temptation to exploit this licence to make money and the coinage was rapidly debased. In type these feudal issues were various, but conservative. The counts of Poitou, who controlled the mines of Melle, continued a type of Charles the Bald (840—77) without even changing the name [figure 79], until Richard Coeur de Lion became count in 1169. In Maine [figure 95], the monogram of Count Herbert I (1016—36), after remaining unchanged for more than two centuries, was finally adorned with fleurs-de-lis and transformed into a sort of crown in honour of Charles of Anjou who was granted the fief in 1246. On deniers of the Abbey of St Martin of Tours the Carolingian basilica type evolved into a stylized representation of a Gothic castle, customarily known as a *châtel tournois*, and as such was reincorporated into the royal coinage of France [figure 91] when Philip Augustus took control of Touraine in 1204; it survived as a standard type until 1369. Other great abbeys, like those of Souvigny in the Bourbonnais and St Martial of Limoges, took for their coin-types the heads of their patron saints, copying them perhaps from reliquaries in their possession [figure 84].

The feudalization of the French coinage went so far that from the end of the tenth century to the middle of the twelfth, the Capetians controlled mints only in their own domain, and it was exceptional for coins issued elsewhere to carry even the king's name. In the model feudal state which the crusaders set up in

41

82 France, masse d'or, c. 1296, Philip IV; despite his nickname, 'le roi faux-monnayeur' issued some of the most beautiful coins of the High Middle Ages [twice actual size].

Outremer, the same system obtained even more rigidly. The king of Jerusalem was only the first of the four great barons of the Holy Land, and there was no question of his having any minting rights within the territories of the other three, the counts of Edessa and Tripoli [figure 86] and the princes of Antioch. According to the Assizes of Jerusalem, even within the kingdom itself some twenty tenants-in-chief had the right to strike coins. The types of the crusaders' silver coins were usually Frankish, but they struck gold coins in imitation of the Saracens, and in Edessa and Antioch, where there was a large Greek population, they also struck bronze coins in the Byzantine manner.

The Holy Roman Emperors [figure 88] did not begin to give away their sovereign rights until the middle of the tenth century, and they were not seriously diminished until after the struggle between Empire and Papacy in the late eleventh century. In Germany it was mostly the great feudatories [figure 73], abbeys, bishops and secular princes who obtained, whether by usurpation or formal grant, the *jus monetae*. In Italy, although the emperors made frequent grants of minting rights to bishops in the twelfth century, in practice control usually fell into the hands of the communes, which were then emerging independently as the most active economic force in Europe [figure 107].

A feature of the German coinage in the twelfth century and later is the unusual fabric of the pieces struck in the eastern provinces. These coins, now called *bracteates*, were struck on only one face; they are very light and so thin that the design, raised on one side, comes through incuse on the other. The larger ones are very fragile and quite unpractical as currency. The evidence suggests that they were used as a means of taxation, being very frequently demonetized in order that the lord might enjoy the impost on a recoinage, which in those parts of the Empire was much heavier than elsewhere. Bad though they were as money, bracteates, being generally much broader than ordinary deniers, gave more scope to the die-engraver, and they were among the few coins of the Romanesque period to reflect its artistic style [figures 73 and 89]. The ecclesiastical issues especially have much in common with contemporary bas-reliefs, both in subject matter and in their designs, often set in an architectural framework. The secular pieces often have a chivalric device, either primitive heraldry or a representation of the lord himself, armed and sometimes mounted.

The revival of European commerce in the eleventh century was closely bound up with Venetian sea-power in the Levant. Venetian merchants established quarters in Constantinople, where they enjoyed customs exemptions which even the emperor's own subjects did not enjoy. The later denari of Venice were quite inadequate for commerce on a grand scale, but as long as the Empire dominated the partnership the medium of exchange

83 Ildebrandino Pagliaresi, chamberlain of the commune of Siena in 1264, making up the public accounts with a bag of silver grossi: a painting on the wooden cover of the public account book.

was Byzantine. Later however the imperial currency degenerated, and after the Fourth Crusade the mastery passed firmly into the hands of the Venetians, who found themselves obliged to start a more valuable coinage of their own. The *grosso*, first issued by the Doge Enrico Dandolo in about 1202, was quite a small silver coin, but it had a value of twenty-four old denari. Its style was purely Byzantine, Christ enthroned on one side and St Mark and the doge on the other, standing stiffly side by side in a pose familiar since the time of Heraclius. The Venetian initiative in the issue of grossi was followed during the next fifty years by most of the other cities of northern and central Italy.

87 (right) Twelfth-century capital in the abbey of Souvigny, showing monks making coins.

84 Souvigny, base silver denier, twelfth/thirteenth-century (the head is that of St Mayeul, an early abbot of Cluny). The mint of this Cluniac abbey was one of the most prolific in France [actual size].

85 England, silver penny, Eustace Fitzjohn, c. 1140; royal control over the coinage broke down in England only in the reign of Stephen. Eustace was a northern baron who fought against Stephen at the Battle of the Standard [actual size].

86 Tripoli, silver gros, Count Bohemond VI of Antioch (1268-74); the crusaders rigidly adhered to the principle of feudal coinage [actual size].

The commercial links of Sicily and southern Italy were traditionally with Byzantium and Islam. In the eleventh and twelfth centuries, when the denier was the common currency of the rest of western Europe, the Norman kings were coining in bronze, the habitual currency of the region, lifting their coin types in the Norman fashion from their predecessors, Arab, Byzantine and even Greek [figures 92 and 93]. They also coined in gold, copying the Saracens. Then in 1231 the Emperor Frederick II, who had inherited the southern kingdom through his mother Constance, issued from his mints at Messina and Brindisi a new gold coin, which foreshadowed economically the gold coinage of modern Europe and artistically the medals and coins of the Renaissance. Frederick's portrait, which appears on it, is not realistic in quite the Renaissance manner, but the die-engraver has carefully observed Roman portrait-coins: the aptly named *augustale* is a remarkable mediaeval expression of the classical ideal [figure 107]. Like Frederick himself, however, this coin was phenomenal but not influential. It was copied only once, thirty-five years later, at the mints of Barletta, Brindisi and Messina for Charles of Anjou [figure 107], and then it was mis-interpreted, its antique spirit overlaid by heraldic trappings.

It was not with the anachronism of Frederick but in the currencies of the trading cities of northern Italy that European gold coinage really began. In 1252 the republic of Genoa issued a gold coin of ten *soldi* to compete with the Saracen *dinars* and Norman *taris* which circulated in the western Mediterranean. Later the same year the Florentine republic minted the first gold *florin* [figure 107], which like the silver florin created rather earlier had a lily (*flos*) as its device, a play on the name of the city after which it was called. Venice was inexplicably late in the field, issuing its

89 Holy Roman Empire, silver bracteate, Frederick Barbarossa (1152-90), mint of Saalfeld [twice actual size].

90 France, écu d'or c.1270, Louis IX; this was the first French gold coin since the Merovingian period. Only eight are known to exist [twice actual size].

first gold coin [figure 107] in 1284, by which time the Byzantine gold which it supplanted in the Levant was utterly decrepit. The designs of the new coin, which were to remain essentially unchanged until the fall of the Venetian republic in 1797, still showed strong Byzantine influence, but the pose of the doge kneeling before St Mark was more relaxed than the hieratic stance of the same two figures on the grosso. Both gold and silver *ducats,* as the Venetian coins were called in allusion to the constitution of the republic, were copied along the sea-routes to the east, in Serbia [figure 98] and the Latin Orient, and by the Arabs. Florentine trade, by contrast, was mostly northward, particularly along the trade routes of the Rhine and the Rhône, so the imitators of the florin who appeared in the fourteenth century were mostly transalpine: the counts of Provence and Flanders, the dukes of Austria, Brabant and Aquitaine and the kings of Aragon and Bohemia.

In northern Europe gold coinage did not begin without difficulty. The experimental issue of a gold penny by Henry III of England in 1257 was soon discontinued. A few years later Louis IX introduced gold coinage to France as part of a larger monetary reform designed to extend the scope of the royal at the expense of the feudal coinage, but the *écu d'or* [figure 90] was the only part of the scheme which seems to have failed. It was probably under-valued at the rate of ten *sous tournois,* and Philip III, who succeeded Louis in 1270, did not proceed with it. The *gros tournois,* a large silver coin of good metal, which was issued in 1266 tariffed at twelve *deniers tournois,* was at once a success. It was struck in large quantities in the next sixty years and soon found imitators in the Low Countries and Germany. Its main type was the conventional *châtel tournois* derived from the Abbey of St Martin, but its concentric design was probably

91 France, silver gros tournois, 1266-70, Louis IX; the first French silver coin larger than a denier; the concentric design may be of Saracen inspiration, but the stylized building on the reverse derives from the basilica of Louis the Pious (see figure 78) [twice actual size].

92 *(above)* Rhegium, silver tetradrachm, c. 445–435 BC [twice actual size].

94 *(right)* England, gold florin, 1344, Edward III, a false start for the English gold coinage. Only two of these are known. They were found together in the river Tyne in 1857 [enlarged 4 : 1].

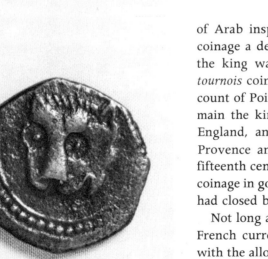

93 Sicily, bronze follaro, William II (1166-89); a local find of Rhegine tetradrachms, sixteen hundred years old, must have inspired this design [twice actual size].

of Arab inspiration [figure 91]. Its popularity gave the royal coinage a decided advantage over the feudal competition, and the king was at some pains to defend his monopoly in the *tournois* coinage, especially against his own brother, Alphonse, count of Poitou, who was quick to produce a copy of it. In the main the king succeeded. In Aquitaine, held by the kings of England, and in such big fiefs and appanages as Burgundy, Provence and Brittany, feudal issues continued well into the fifteenth century, some of them in blatant imitation of the royal coinage in gold and silver; but the great majority of feudal mints had closed by 1300.

Not long after Louis IX had established the good name of the French currency, his grandson Philip IV lost it by tampering with the alloy and the official value of the various coins. In fact Philip succeeded where Louis had failed in establishing a gold coinage, but his alterations set a bad precedent which his Valois

95 *(opposite)* A nineteenth-century copy of a thirteenth-century window in Le Mans Cathedral showing money changers with a customer; the coins on the tables in the foreground are probably feudal deniers of Le Mans.

96 Bohemia, silver groschen, Wenceslas II; this coin, first minted in 1300, bears witness to the eastward extension of economic activity in Europe. The groschen of Prague became a staple silver coin in central Europe [enlarged $1\frac{1}{4}$: 1].

97 Cyprus, silver gros, Henry II (1310-24) [actual size].

98 Serbia, silver grosso, Stephen IV Dragutin (1272-1316); a special office was set up in Venice to deal with these coins. Only St Stephen, substituted for St Mark (though he still holds the evangelist's gospel), and the king's name distinguish these coins from Venetian grossi [actual size].

successors followed to the limit in the next century. It is paradoxical that Philip, nicknamed *le roi faux-monnayeur*, should have issued the most beautiful series of coins of the High Middle Ages [figure 82]. Gothic art, which had so far scarcely touched coinage anywhere, suddenly appears fully developed in his gold, especially in the delicate framework of tracery and lettering in which the king is shown enthroned with all the attributes of royalty. These coins have little subtlety of modelling in their low relief, but the two-dimensional patterns are so rich that they almost give an illusion of colour. Indeed, unlike most coins, this Gothic gold has more affinity with contemporary miniature painting than with sculpture, a characteristic which becomes even more marked with the great flowering of heraldic designs in the next century.

The century of the Black Death and the Hundred Years' War was not, like the thirteenth, a period of great economic advance. The frontiers were pushed forward a little, especially in the direction of the mining country of Bohemia, where in 1300 King Wenceslas II introduced a new silver *groschen* which quickly became a leading trading currency in central Europe [figure 96]. In Germany, where the co-operation of the Hanseatic League set an example in counteracting some of the economic consequences of the fragmentation of the Empire, the princes of several areas such as the Rhineland set up monetary unions to standardize the type and weight of their version of the gold florin or *gulden*. In Italy the traditional currencies continued, and one was added in the south by Charles II of Anjou who in 1303 issued a new silver coin, the *gigliato*. This was larger than the grossi of northern Italy, and indeed looked very French with its Gothic design of the king enthroned. It was widely traded in the Mediterranean for a hundred and fifty years and was copied with crude but vigorous effect by the Lusignan kings of Cyprus [figure 97]. It was also copied in Hungary, where another Angevin, Charles Robert (1308–42) preferred the example of his Neapolitan cousin to that of his Bohemian neighbour.

Learning from their experience in Italy as rivals and successors of the Angevins, the kings of Aragon were not slow to reform the coinage of their Spanish dominions. The fine silver grossi of Barcelona, first struck by Peter III (1276–85) and the workaday gold florins, dating from the reign of Peter IV (1336–87), illustrate the activity of Catalan trade in the Mediterranean at that time. They also present a healthy contrast to Castile, still preoccupied with the *reconquista*, where the issue of a few magnificent gold coins and quantities of debased silver is suggestive of an over-privileged nobility and an over-taxed people.

In France the silver was terribly debased by the hard-pressed Valois, and the gold underwent frequent alterations. But although the economic importance of France declined, the prestige

99 *(top row)* Flanders, franc à cheval and demi-lion, Louis de Mâle (1346–84); *(bottom row)* Flanders, heaume d'or and lion d'or (reverse), Louis de Mâle; Hainault, double royal, William III (1356-89). The coins of fourteenth-century Flanders and Hainault make an exuberant display of late Gothic art [actual size].

100 The fourteenth-century Hôtel de la Monnaie at Figeac in Aquitaine. Figeac was a royal mint from 1346, but it was ceded to Edward III of England from 1358. The only coins which can be identified as having been made here are some of the Black Prince.

101 France, écu d'or à la couronne, 1445–7, Charles VII; the écu, or crown, was the standard French gold coin from 1385 to 1640 [actual size].

103 France, salut d'or, 1446-9, Henry VI of England, mint of Rouen; an elegant combination of religious sentiment and politically charged heraldry [actual size].

102 Burying coins was a common practice in the middle ages, especially in time of war. Most surviving mediaeval coins come from the hoards that their owners never came back to collect (from a fifteenth-century French manuscript of Boethius).

104 Aquitaine, silver demi-gros, Edward the Black Prince (1362-72), minted at Figeac; the initial 'F' appears just to the left above the prince's head [actual size].

105 A pair of dies for a groat of Edward III (1327–77): on the left the reverse die or trussle, which was held in a pair of pincers and hammered; on the right the obverse die or pile, which was set by its spike in the anvil [see figure 70].

of her civilization was still shown in the designs of the gold, which in some cases was decorated with such a profusion of heraldry and tracery that the actual field of the coin was dissolved altogether like the wall surface of a Gothic church. The chivalric aspirations of King John the Good were given spirited expression in the design of the *franc à cheval* [figure 99], the first coin of its name, which was issued in such great numbers to pay John's ransom after Poitiers. After that the establishment in 1385 of the *écu d'or* as the standard gold coin, with its plain shield of arms, comes as an anti-climax [figure 101].

England's coinage during the Hundred Years' War was less varied than that of her antagonist, but healthier. In 1344, after a false start with a gold florin [figure 94] of twice the weight of the Italian coin, which was over-valued at six shillings and so rejected, a viable gold coinage was established with the *noble*, a larger coin valued at 6s 8d. The obverse type of the king in the ship may have been an allusion to the recent naval victory at Sluys, but, even if not, it was an apt symbol of England's aggressive spirit just before Crécy [figure 106]. The style was coarser than that of the best French work or of the florin. The strength of the coinage, however, was shown in the silver. Although diminished in weight, the sterling still preserved enough of its value to continue as a standard trading counter, and not until 1351 was it even found necessary to extend its

106 England, gold noble, 1360-9, Edward III; this was the standard English gold coin for more than a century. The type may commemorate the naval victory at Sluys [actual size].

51

107 *(top to bottom)* Brindisi, augustale, *c. 1231*, Emperor Frederick II; Barletta, augustale, *c. 1266*, Charles I of Anjou; Venice, ducat, Giovanni Dandolo (1280–89); Florence, florin, *c. 1252*, obverse and reverse. Some of the earliest gold coins of mediaeval Italy, including the first ducat and the first florin [slightly enlarged].

range with a *groat* of fourpence. The types and fineness of the silver were unchanged until the sixteenth century, but there was some modification in the appearance of the gold in the reign of Edward IV, when the value of the noble was raised to ten shillings.

Except for the sterling and its multiples, which must have been useful for paying English soldiers, the Plantagenets did not impose coinage of English type in Aquitaine but, once the noble was established, they ensured that much of their gold coinage in France conformed to English weight standards. Most of their silver was local in character, but the coins which could be used in external trade were generally English in content though French in appearance. The same principle was followed when after 1422 Henry VI, as king of France, controlled the greater part of the French national coinage and not just a provincial one. His elegant *salut d'or* [figure 103], which weighed half a noble and the same as the florin, was a formidable rival to the écu.

England's economic importance in the late Middle Ages was as a supplier of raw materials to Flemish industry. Flemish cloth was the chief commodity in European trade and the staple outward cargo of Venetian and Hanseatic merchantmen. As an industrial region, attracting traders rather than sending them out like the Italian communes, the Low Countries received large quantities of foreign coin, and their own coinage took on a typically European as distinct from national character. Territorially the Netherlands were attached to France and the Empire, but economically they were associated with Italy, England and the Rhineland. The coinage was open to every influence, and although until the middle of the fourteenth century the kings of France tried to impose their own monetary system on Flanders, whose count was a peer of France, the various provinces in fact borrowed from their neighbours whatever suited them best, the sterling, the gros, the florin, the noble, the franc [figure 99] and the royal. In many instances the designs of these coins closely followed their prototypes but others were evidently intended to assert the issuers' sovereignty. Frequent recoinage provided the feudal lords with a useful means of taxing the bourgeoisie and the types therefore were often changed. Moreover, the Flemings were rich and required big coins, the double of everything, double gros and double royal [figure 99]. Their coinage therefore gave scope for a varied display of late Gothic art. That of Count Louis de Mâle of Flanders is the most magnificent of the whole mediaeval series, richer though less refined than that of the Valois, while the counts of Hainault issued a few coins in less exuberant taste which excel even the best French work of the period. The coins of this small group of provinces provide a full commentary on the economic life of late mediaeval Europe and illustrate the last extravagant phase of its art.

THE RENAISSANCE AND THE BAROQUE

108 Austria, thaler, 1518, Emperor Maximilian I; an early German portrait coin of the Renaissance [twice actual size].

WHEN THE BYZANTINE EMPEROR John VIII Palaeologus came to Italy in 1438 to seek in vain at the Council of Ferrara the aid of the Pope against the Turks, his visit was marked by the striking of a portrait medal by the Veronese painter, Pisanello. A conservative among painters, Pisanello was an innovator as a medallist. Although there is something of the fantastic spirit of his pictures in the curious hat which the emperor is wearing on this, the first of Pisanello's medals, under the hat is portrayed a man, closely observed and delicately modelled [figure 109]. The form, interesting in itself and lifelike, contrasts strongly with the stylized figures and decorative patterns of mediaeval coins, and still more with the caricatures of the traditional images of divine and imperial power which appear on John's own coinage at Constantinople.

110 *(left)* Milan, silver testone, Bona of Savoy, regent for Gian Galeazzo Maria Sforza (1476-81); the increasing size of coins gave more scope for design and portraiture [actual size].

113 *(right)* Milan, silver testone, Ludovico Maria Sforza (1494–1500); the last Sforza duke of Milan portrayed by the medallist Caradosso [actual size].

111 *(left)* Ferrara, silver testone, c. 1503, Ercole I d'Este; the equestrian figure on the reverse may be derived from Leonardo da Vinci's statue of Francesco Sforza, now destroyed [actual size].

112 Milan, gold double ducat, Gian Galeazzo Maria Sforza; one of the most charming of early Renaissance coins [actual size].

109 *(opposite)* Bronze medal by Pisanello commemorating the presence of the Byzantine Emperor John VIII Palaeologus at the Council of Ferrara in 1438.

It was twenty-five years before the style of Pisanello's medals worked through to coinage. The depth of relief on which Pisanello's technique was based could only be achieved on a broad thick flan. His medals were not struck, but cast, a method which in recent times has been considered unsuitable for coinage in any quantity. Moreover, in the middle of the fifteenth century there was neither the metal available nor the economic need for big coins, and there was in any case a reaction against earlier artistic developments.

An obvious feature of the new humanism as applied to coinage was the way in which it gave publicity to the character of the ruler himself as distinct from his office. It is not surprising therefore that the first to apply it was Francesco Sforza, Duke of Milan (1450–66), whose power was based on no dynastic claim but on his intellectual and physical prowess and the force of his personality.

The small module of Francesco's ducats permitted only a limited use of relief, and his coins are pretty but not wholly successful. His son, Galeazzo Maria, struck larger and finer coins, the double ducat in gold and the silver *testone*, so called from the prominence of the portrait head. After Galeazzo Maria's assassination in 1476, the coinage of the Sforza reflects the family's changing fortunes: first comes the widowed duchess as guardian for her infant son [figure 110], then the son, Gian Galeazzo Maria,

114 Scotland, silver groat, James III (1460-88); an isolated instance of early Renaissance influence in northern Europe [twice actual size].

115 Naples, silver carlino, 1503, Ferdinand of Aragon and Isabella of Castile; because of the dynastic connection, Renaissance influences came to Spain by way of Naples [actual size].

116 England, silver testoon or shilling, c. 1507-9, Henry VII [actual size].

a ravishing long-haired little boy wearing a skull cap [figure 112]. In 1481, on a series of double ducats and testoni, the work of Caradosso, the youthful grace of Gian Galeazzo is contrasted with the grim features of his uncle, Ludovico il Moro, who first appears on the reverse. The stronger wins, and on the last coins of the Sforza, among the most plentiful as well as beautiful of the Renaissance, Ludovico is alone [figure 113].

Others soon followed the example of the Sforza. Borso d'Este, Duke of Ferrara (1450–71) and Ludovico Gonzaga, Marquis of Mantua (1444–78), the patron of Mantegna, were among the earliest, and coin-portraiture developed further under their successors. Especially distinguished were the coins of Ercole I of Ferrara (1471–1505), the reverses of which also show completely new forms [figure 111], and of his son Alfonso I. The Mantuan dynasty was to maintain a tradition of beautiful coins for nearly two hundred years [figure 130], among the most remarkable being the early coins of Francesco II (1484–1519) who married Isabella d'Este and held the most refined court in Italy [figure 124].

Many lesser Italian princes wished to achieve the distinction of a portrait-coinage. Typical of these, Giovanni II Bentivoglio, Lord of Bologna (1449–1509), who earlier had issued no coins of his own out of respect to his suzerain the Pope, seized the opportunity of a licence given to him in 1494 as part of a political manoeuvre by the Emperor Maximilian. His double ducats and testoni enhanced his prestige, and are now his chief memorial [figure 123].

The Popes themselves were not deterred by the self-glorification implicit in the issue of a portrait-coinage at this time. Sixtus IV was portrayed on a double grosso and the Borgia Alexander VI issued a great piece of three ducats in commemoration of the Jubilee Year 1500. The revival of the Roman practice of commemorative issues was in itself typical of the Renaissance. Its continuation has been a chief characteristic of the Papal coinage ever since.

While so many changes were taking place, the coinages of Venice and Florence, which were by far the most important in Italy, remained quite unaltered. Their very importance partly accounts for this. The florin and the ducat were not only current all over Italy; they were the staple of foreign exchange throughout Europe and the Mediterranean world. This position had been built up through more than two centuries, and they had remained virtually unchanged in standard and design. It was thought, no doubt, that to transform the coins' appearance would jeopardize their carefully guarded reputations. So in 1500, when most Italian states were producing fine coins in the new idiom, the coinages of the two cities which took the lead in most fields of artistic development were archaic and sterile, like that of

117 A Flemish banker
and his wife, 1520; an oil
painting by Quentin Metsys,
now in the Louvre.

57

118 Tyrol, silver guldengroschen, 1486, Sigismund; the first of the large silver coins of central Europe [actual size].

Athens eighteen centuries earlier. At Venice and Florence political motives may also have been behind the preservation of the old forms. The Venetian republic jealously suppressed any form of personal aggrandizement, while at Florence the Medici still encouraged the fiction that they were no more than private citizens. A portrait-coinage would have accorded with neither the principles of the one nor the pretences of the other.

The Italian influence was slow to make itself felt in the coinage of other countries. There were exceptions, a notably early one being the isolated appearance in Scotland in 1485 of a refined three-quarter-face portrait on a groat of James III [figure 114]; but in the early years of the sixteenth century the coinage of Europe still wore a predominantly mediaeval aspect [figure 146]. There were modifications, refinements in the treatment of traditional mofifs, such as occurred, for example, on the English *angel*, where St Michael's angular Gothic pose gave way to one

119 England, gold sovereign, Henry VII (1485–1509); a new English coin, the name and style of which are both suggestive of the Tudors' attitude to monarchy. The obverse design was derived from a Flemish original [twice acual size]

more relaxed and natural; but far-reaching changes in design were mostly kept for new denominations.

The kings of Naples had struck portrait coins since 1485 at least, but their style, overlaid with the trappings of royalty, was not altogether in the humanist idiom [figure 115]. A version of this was transported to Spain when Ferdinand and Isabella, who were also king and queen of Naples, reformed the Castilian coinage in 1497. Their profile portraits on the gold *excelente* and its multiples were evidently based on Neapolitan models, but their face-to-face pose was a new revival of a Roman motif [figure 146]. In the sixteenth century it was much copied on the coins of other married heiresses, notably Mary Tudor, Mary Queen of Scots and Joan of Navarre.

120 and 121 *(above)* Zurich, silver thaler, 1512 (the patron saints of the city, Felix, Regula and Exuperantius); *(right)* Sitten (Switzerland), silver 1½ thalers, 1501, Bishop Matthäus Schiner (St Theodul praying between an angel and a devil). Two picturesque, but overloaded designs typical of the first thaler-sized coins [both twice actual size].

122 Scotland, gold 20 pound piece, 1576, James VI; the art of striking fine coins by the old hammered method surived longest in the remoter and less active European mints, such as Edinburgh [actual size].

Just as the illegitimate dynasties of Italy had the more quickly adopted portrait-coinage in order to enhance their prestige, so in northern Europe the Tudor Henry VII took up the new idea well before Louis XII in France, even though Louis had from the first struck portrait pieces for his Italian territories. The traditional full-face effigy on the English silver was gradually transformed under Henry VII, until by 1504 the features had become quite recognizably those of the reigning king. Then, in 1507, a complete change was made to a profile portrait [figure 116]. This was adopted for the groat, the half groat and for an experimental new denomination, the *testoon,* worth a shilling. The significance of the portrait seems however to have been rather lost on the English, because for seventeen years after he succeeded in 1509, Henry VIII retained his father's likeness.

In gold the chief innovation of Henry VII was the *sovereign* of twenty shillings. Its design, on the obverse the king enthroned, as on certain coins of Maximilian in the Netherlands, and on the reverse a shield of arms set in a rose, although still essentially in the mediaeval tradition, was touched with the vigour and something also of the vulgarity of the new age [figure 119].

Despite his early experience in Italy, Louis XII only introduced the teston to France in 1514; it was tariffed at first at ten sous. Inferior in style to the excellent pieces made for Louis fourteen years earlier as Duke of Milan, the first French testons had much in common with the silver coins of Henry VII. The common characteristics of the two coinages became much more marked

59

123 and 124 (top) Bologna, double ducat, Giovanni II Bentivoglio (1494-1506); (bottom) Mantua, double ducat, Francesco II Gonzaga (1484-1519). Two early Renaissance portrait coins [enlarged 3:1].

125 and 126 *(top)* Brabant, philippsdaalder, 1557, Philip II; *(bottom)* Mexico, 8 reales, Philip II, reverse. Silver from America, in the form of bullion or roughly made pieces of eight, flooded into Spain in the sixteenth century; this wealth was mortgaged by Philip to pay for his foreign commitments, and much of it found its way to the Netherlands [twice actual size].

when in 1526 Henry VIII introduced the *crown* as a standard coin in imitation of the French écu. At about the same time coinage of the Low Countries was adapted with more versatility to meet the requirements of trade with both France and the Empire, when Charles V incorporated in the common currency of the provinces a *couronne d'or* after the pattern of the écu as well as the florin after the German model.

Towards the end of the fifteenth century, the discovery of new mines and the more active exploitation of old ones in the mountain ranges of Saxony and Bohemia, led to a big increase in the silver supply, which was to transform the coinage of Germany. As early as 1486 Archduke Sigismund of Tyrol struck a large silver coin of the value of a gold florin or gulden and known therefore as a *guldengroschen* [figure 118] The Emperor Maximilian I was among the many who imitated this coin [figure 108]. Then in 1520 the counts of Schlick in Bohemia, who had rich mines at Joachimsthal, began to strike similar coins of slightly lower alloy. These coins, which had great success and circulated widely, were known from their place of origin as *joachimsthalers*. Shortened to *thaler*, the name was soon given to other coins of the same size and standard. Outside Germany the name was commonly applied to any big silver coin, as in the form *dollar* it still is.

At first the thaler had the advantage that it did not come under the more or less effective control which the imperial authority had exercised over the issue of gold since 1442. Charles V attempted to regulate the large silver, incidentally trying to restrict the issue of thalers to those authorities who actually controlled silver mines. His regulations were not generally obeyed, but in 1559 the Emperor Ferdinand I promulgated a system which was fairly widely accepted. The imperial authority, operating through the Diet, was in no position to enforce regulations in detail, and the coinage was only preserved from utter disorder by the association of the various issuing authorities, the princes, bishops and free imperial cities, into local 'circles' which agreed to keep to a common standard and accounting system. The Empire was divided into ten of these, but Prussia and Bohemia stood aloof. Small change remained virtually unregulated and a source of much profit to the issuers.

The large flan of the thaler provided a promising field for the die-engraver. Sigismund's coin of 1486 displayed the purely mediaeval design of the armed horseman to great advantage. On the portrait-coins, which show a strong Italian influence, ideal beauty was often sacrificed for a more trenchant realism, but at least the subject was at first given the centre of the field unencumbered [figure 108]. Temperamentally, however, the German engravers preferred the picturesque, and their tendency was to overlay the design with a mass of detail [figures 120 and

127 France, silver ½ franc, 1591, the League, Toulouse. The Leaguers in Toulouse refused to recognize Henry IV, but had no candidate for the throne themselves; they therefore continued with a portrait of Henry III, assassinated in 1589 [actual size].

128 *(opposite)* A mint during the reign of the Emperor Maximilian I (1493-1519) from the *Weisskunig.*

62

LEVRS ALTEZES SER.mes NOS PRINCES SOVVERAINS

desirans qu'vn chascun ait cognoissance des pieces d'or & d'argent nouuelles, n'agueres ordon-
nees, & qu'à present l'on forge aux nom, tiltre, armes & figures d'icelles, ont voulu, & commande
aux Maistres Generaulx de leurs Monnoyes de pardeça, de faire imprimer les figures desdictes pieces tant
d'or que d'argent, auec declaration de leur pris & poix qui est tel comme s'enfuit.

VNe piece d'or nommee le doubl Souuerain, de hault a-
loy pefant vn esterlins ix. aes efars au pris de xij florins
ou xl. folz de gros, monnoye de Flandres la piece.

VNe piece d'Argent de haut aloy nommee le Souuerain
d'argēt, pefant xviij. esterlins xiiij. aes, au pris de xlviij pat.
ou viij. folz de Flandres la piece.

LE fengle Souuerain de mefme aloy des doubles reaulx d'or
cy deuant forgez, par feu l'Empereur Charles V. de tres
haulte memoire, & Philippe le Roy Catholique d'Efpaigne,
pefant iij. efterlins xij. aes & demy efcars au pris de vi. florins,
ou xx. folz de Flandres la piece.

VNe autre de mefme haut aloy eftant la moitie dudict Souuerain pefant ix. efterlins, vij. aes & au pris de xxiiij. patarts
ou iiij. fols de Flandres la piece.

DOubles tiers dudict Souuerain pareillemēt d'or fin, pefans
ij.efterlins ix. aes efcars au pris de iiij. florins ou xij. fols iiij.
deniers gros dicte monnoye de Flandres la piece.

VNe autre d'argent pareillement de mefme haut aloy eftant
le quart dudict Souuerain, pefant iiij. efterlins xix. & demy
aes efcars, au pris de xij. pat. ou deux fols de Flandres la piece.

DEmy Souuerain d'aloy comme lefdictz doubles & le poix
à l'aduenant, au pris de trois florins, ou x. fols de gros la piece, monnoye de Flandres.

SEngles fols de moindre aloy eftans le viij. part dudict Souuerain pefans trois efterlins xiiij. & demy aes, au pris de fix pat.
la piece.

LE nouueau Patart pefant vn efterlin
viij. aes, qui fe allouera pour vn pat.
ou deux gros de Flandres la piece.

LE nouueau demy Patart, pefant vingt
& vn aes, & vn quart, qui fe allouera
pour vn demy patart ou vn gros de Flandres la piece.

LE Liart ou quart dudict Patart le poix
à l'aduenant: dudict demy Patart qui fe
allouera pour vn Lyart ou douze mites
de Flandres la piece.

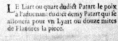

Le tout aux remedes accoutumez & à l'aduenant, & fe fur autres pieces femblables eft ordonné & accordé.

A ANVERS
Chez Hierofme Verduffen, Imprimeur de la Monnoye de leurs Altezes Sereniffimes
noz Princes Souuerains. 1612.   Auecq grace & Priuilege.

130 Mantua, 8 doppie, Carlo II during the regency of his mother, Maria Gonzaga (1637-47); the widow's veil of the regent provides an unusual opportunity for this exercise in baroque design [twice actual size].

129 *(opposite)* Official handbill issued in Antwerp in 1612 describing the type, weight and value of the coinage of the Archdukes Albert and Isabella for the Spanish Netherlands.

121]. The direction taken by German heraldry at this time contributed to the overcrowding, as even the thaler was scarcely big enough for the proper display of all the quarterings and crests of a German nobleman [figure 143].

In Italy the freshness of vision for which the early coins were remarkable later gave way to a more conscious imitation of the antique [figure 139]. 'Your Holiness can boast of a currency superior to any of the ancients', said the Pope's secretary in 1529, after Benvenuto Cellini was appointed by Clement VII to be *maestro delle stampe* at the papal mint. In 1535 Benvenuto went to Florence where he engraved dies for Duke Alessandro, the first of the Medici to issue a portrait-coinage there [figure 139]. His coins for both Clement and Alessandro are, it must be confessed, disappointing: their general effect is flat, and there is none of the subtle sensitivity which distinguishes his other work in metal. It may be that he strove for an effect too fine for his medium. His rival, Leone Leoni, whom he later accused of being basely involved in a plot to poison him with powdered diamonds

131 Jean Varin showing an antique medal to
the young Louis XIV.

132 France, double henri d'or à la Gallie,
1553–8, Henry II, reverse; this rare coin,
minted at the Moulin des Étuves in Paris,
shows the strong influence of imperial Rome on
French medallists of the mid-sixteenth century
[twice actual size].

when he was in the Pope's prison of St Angelo, achieved a far
grander effect with bold, almost Roman relief on dies which he
made for Charles V at Milan [figure 139].

The same features that were idealized by Leone Leoni at Milan
were treated with a brutal realism on the big silver florin which
Charles V introduced in the Netherlands as a rival to the thaler.
Large coins began to proliferate at this time as the heavy influx
of gold and silver from America began to tell on the European
economy. Coming first to Spain, most of the metal went through
it, like water through a sieve, to pay for the king of Spain's
heavy foreign commitments, especially in the Netherlands
[figures 125 and 126]. The increase in the money supply led to
a rapid expansion of domestic and foreign trade and to a sharp
rise in prices. Even the more plentiful precious metals went up
in price as governments, hard pressed for funds, cried up the
value now of their gold and now of their silver coins. Throughout
Europe there was a continuous rise in the number of coins and in
their value in terms of money of account, accompanied by a
steady fall in their purchasing power. For example in France the
écu, tariffed at $36\frac{1}{4}$ sous tournois in 1515, rose by stages to 75 s.t.
in 1614, despite successive reductions in size, while the teston
rose from 10 s.t. in 1515 to $14\frac{1}{2}$ s.t. in 1575, when it was superseded by the franc.

The social and political consequences of the inflation were
grave and far-reaching. In the narrow field of coinage the immediate problems raised were those of manufacture and or-

133 Rome, silver scudo, 1699, Innocent XII; a work of the German engraver G. Hamerani [actual size].

ganization. The workmanship of the mints deteriorated as pressure mounted. Busy mints, such as that at Antwerp, where a great quantity of American silver was recoined, put out particularly shabby pieces, ill-struck and often split in the process. Only in the remote mints, like that of Edinburgh, were the old-fashioned standards of craftsmanship fully maintained until late in the century [figure 122].

The remedy lay in the use of coining machinery, but although the invention, perfected in Augsburg, was first hawked round the courts of Europe in the 1550's, it was bitterly opposed by the closed shop of the moneyers' guilds and was not commonly accepted for nearly a hundred years. In 1551 Henry II of France established by letters patent the *Moulin des Étuves* under the direction of Guillaume de Marillac. Installed at the western end of the Île du Palais, it was equipped with a rolling mill, powered by the waters of the Seine, for reducing the metal to its proper thickness, a mechanical cutter for making the blanks and a screw-press for the actual striking. The superiority of the new method over the hand process can be seen from the coins them-

134 Newark, England, silver ninepence, 1646, Charles I; the royalist fortress on the Trent issued large quantities of this lozenge-shaped money [actual size].

135 Leyden, Holland, paper 28 stuivers, 1574; a relic of the famous siege by the Spaniards, when the city was reduced to issuing coins made of paper [actual size].

136 Urbino, silver ½ scudo, 1705, Pope Clement XI, reverse; this view of Urbino is the most ambitious of all medallic exercises in perspective [twice actual size].

137 France, 8 louis d'or, obverse, and 10 louis d'or, reverse, 1640, Louis XIII; these large gold coins were among the first to be struck by Jean Varin using the new machinery at the Louvre [twice actual size].

selves, which are round, well centred and evenly struck up [figure 132]. In design a reinterpretation of Roman models after the later Italian fashion, the productions of the new mint were among the best of their time. However, the vested interests of the established moneyers prevailed, and after 1562 the *Moulin des Étuves* was taken off regular coinage work. Later it was briefly employed for coinage again, not by the king of France this time, but by Henry of Navarre to strike coins for his territory of Béarn. It was finally suppressed as a mint in 1585.

In England the experiment ended more disastrously. In 1561 Eloi Mestrel, whose name suggests that he was a Huguenot, was authorized to set up in the Tower of London machinery such as that used in Paris. The coins which he made are neat and pretty, remarkable particularly for their lettering, which is the best on any English coins. Nevertheless, the Warden of the Mint complained that his work was slow, expensive and ill-done, and in 1572 he was discharged. Eloi then took to coining on his own account, and in 1578 he was hanged for it at Norwich.

138 England, silver crown, 1663, Charles II. The most famous of English coins: Thomas Simon's 'Petition Crown' which he presented to the king as a protest against his replacement at the mint by Jan Roettiers [enlarged 3 : 1].

139 (left to right) Florence, testone, Alessandro de'Medici (1533–35), from dies by Benvenuto Cellini; Ferrara, testone, Ercole II d'Este (1534–59); Milan, testone, Emperor Charles V (1535–56), from dies by Leone Leoni. Three coins of the High Renaissance [enlarged $1\frac{1}{2}$: 1].

The other requirement for dealing with the increased output of coinage was the strengthening of mint organization and control. As early as 1520, Charles V had reorganized the Netherlands mints on the basis of one for each province and two for Brabant, all of them coining to the same standard. In 1540 Francis I reformed the French system. Provincial minting was continued, but coins were to be clearly marked with a mint letter, A – Paris, B – Rouen, etc, and all assays were to be made at the *Chambre des Monnaies* in Paris. Under Henry II in 1547, the office of *tailleur général* was instituted to supervise the manufacture of the punches used to make all dies; thenceforward provincial styles disappeared although the coins were minted locally. Thus control was shifted to Paris even though it did not become the sole national mint as London became at about that time.

The mint letters of Francis I were one of the few systems of the *ancien régime* to survive the Revolution: they lasted until the end of the nineteenth century. Indeed the whole organization was remarkably stable, continuing normally even through the War of the League. The question then at issue was who should be king of France, and to the French administrative mind this need imply no irregularity in the coinage. The various parties all used the ordinary types. The royalist towns struck in the name of Henry IV, those in the League for Charles X, Cardinal de Bourbon, and those unwilling to commit themselves, in the name of the dead king Henry III [figure 127]. They used the regular mints, and when obliged to set up an irregular one they did so with all due formality and gave it the most logical mint letter.

The Dutch coinage by contrast was utterly disorganized during the revolt against Philip II. At first the States, still in

140 Piacenza, silver scudo, 1589, Alexander Farnese, Duke of Parma; a fine portrait of the famous governor of the Netherlands, by the medallist Antonio Costino [actual size].

141 Saxony, silver thaler, John George (1611–56); a common coin struck during the Thirty Years' War [actual size].

142 England, silver crown, 1644, Charles I, mint of Oxford; this view of Oxford on a rare pattern by Thomas Rawlins is the only English example of a topographical design [actual size].

143 Brunswick-Wolfenbuttel, silver thaler, 1643, Augustus the Young; the ringing of church bells and the rising sun symbolize the departure of imperial troops during the Thirty Years' War [actual size].

theory loyal to Philip's person, struck coins in his name, but in 1575 the States of Holland struck a piece on their own account, the *leuwendaalder*. Other provinces followed their example, and the attempts of William of Orange and later the Earl of Leicester to impose a unified system, were only partly successful in the face of provincial separatism. A curious feature of William's coinage of 1579, often repeated by the Dutch during the war, was the issue of a noble after the fifteenth-century English type. Eventually the exigencies of trade forced the States to do for themselves what William and Leicester had failed to do, and in 1606 the provinces all conformed to the same standard. Meanwhile the southern provinces had returned to their loyalty to Philip and these provinces reintroduced their pre-war system.

Even the Thirty Years' War could scarcely lead to any greater fragmentation of the German coinage than there had been before. The war started with a period of rapid inflation as the mints flooded the country with base small change, but this wholesale profiteering eventually defeated itself and after four years there was a return to sounder policies. Thalers, the chief use of which at this time was to pay the troops, were issued in the name and with the portrait of most of the war's main protagonists, the emperors of course, the Winter King, Gustavus Adolphus, Christian IV of Denmark, Wallenstein and, commonest of all, John George of Saxony who owned the richest mines [figure 141]. Many coins alluded to the war, some not without a certain rueful humour, like the *glockenthaler* of Augustus the Young of Brunswick-Wolfenbuttel: issued to celebrate the departure of the imperial troops, it showed the ringing of church bells and the legend TANDEM PATIENTIA VICTRIX [figure 143].

In the English Civil War, Parliament, controlling the Tower mint, continued to strike coins in the king's name. No change was made even in the legend CHRISTO AUSPICE REGNO, though this was hardly in line with Parliament's policy. The king, deprived of London, had to set up new mints of his own at Shrewsbury, at Oxford, where he coined quantities of college plate, and at Bristol. Meanwhile his supporters established mints in his name at various towns in the north and west, including Chester, Worcester and Exeter. At his own mints Charles abandoned the pre-war types and legends and replaced them by a bold manifesto: The Protestant Religion, The Laws of England and the Liberties of Parliament. The coins of both Civil War parties are thus a permanent record of their political double-thinking.

The siege was a characteristic feature of warfare at this time, and beleaguered cities, short of money as of other necessities of life, often produced coins of their own. Crudely struck and

144 Joseph Roettiers, who worked at the mints of London and Paris, and became engraver general to Louis XIV in 1682. An engraving by C. Vermeulen from a painting by Largillière.

145 Piacenza, silver scudo, 1626, Odoardo Farnese, Duke of Parma; an early example of baroque coin design, by Luca Xell [actual size].

frequently bearing traces of the domestic plate from which many of them were made, they sometimes give pathetic expression to the feelings of the besieged: *Dieu a veu l'afflision*, the despair of the people of Cambrai; *Post mortem patris pro filio*, the defiance of the royalist Colonel Morris who defended Pontefract even after the execution of Charles I in 1649. There were many sieges and many such coins, among the best known those of Vienna (1529), Haarlem (1572), Leyden (1574) where the defenders were reduced to coining paper missal covers [figure 135], Magdeburg (1629) and Newark (1645/6) [figure 134]. Occasionally, though more rarely, the besieging force was reduced to the same expedient, as happened to M. de Turenne who had to coin his plate to pay his troops before St Venant in Artois in 1657.

The even and certain impression produced by the new method of coining by the screw-press was essential to the elaborate baroque design of seventeenth-century German thalers, even enabling the engravers to realize such ambitious effects of perspective as views of cities, which then became a fashionable motif [figure 136]. German engravers were much in demand even in Italy, where some of the best work was done by such artists as Luca Xell and the Hamerani, who, losing nothing of their native force, learned in their changed environment a new subtlety and refinement [figures 133 and 145].

In France, Nicolas Briot, who held the office of *tailleur général* from 1605 until 1625, tried in vain to re-establish the use of the screw-press. Disappointed, he went to England, where, if he met with little more co-operation from his colleagues, he at least enjoyed enthusiastic royal favour. A precise engraver, working in very low relief, he achieved effects of great delicacy. His own milled pieces were of the highest quality, and even the coarse English hammered coinage was a little improved through his influence.

In 1640 Louis XIII finally established minting machinery at the Louvre, and the opportunity was taken to issue new coins

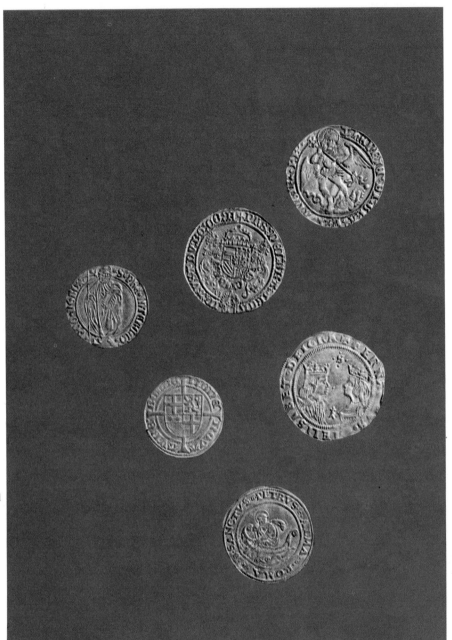

146 *(top to bottom)* England, angel, c. 1500, Henry VII, London mint; Burgundian Netherlands, toison d'or and florin philippus, Philippe le Beau (1494–1506), mints of Bruges and Antwerp; Spain, double excelente, Ferdinand and Isabella (1479–1504), mint of Seville; Cologne, gulden, Archbishop Hermann VI von Hensse (1480–1508), reverse; Rome, double ducat, Alexander VI Borgia (1492–1503), reverse. Six coins that might have been on the counter of an early sixteenth-century Flemish banker [actual size].

including an *écu d'argent*, the first large French silver coin, and a *louis d'or* valued at ten livres, all with the king's portrait: Jean Varin, who engraved the dies for these, is considered by many to be the greatest master who worked for the Paris mint. His bust of Louis is deceptively simple. He achieved all the flowing rhythms of baroque design by means of subtle variations in the modelling of the face, neck and shoulders and without the usual profusion of hair, drapery and armour [figure 137]. The effect is one of grandeur without fuss; even the little piece of five sous is a coin of great dignity.

73

147 Thomas Simon: an eighteenth-century portrait engraving by Vertue.

A few years later Varin only partly succeeded when faced with the task of achieving a similar effect with the chubby features of the five-year-old Louis XIV, but he was luckier in his material than his contemporary and equal Thomas Simon who had to engrave dies for the Commonwealth. Later Simon was commissioned to make patterns for a portrait-coinage of Oliver Cromwell, and he produced magnificent work, a perfect translation of Varin's idiom into English with all of the Frenchman's restraint but an added touch of realism and strength, well suited to the sitter's character [figure 149]. However, the Lord Protector died and the coins never had much circulation. Two years later the Restoration appeared to offer Simon another opportunity of release from Puritan shackles. He did some charming patterns of coins for Charles II, but for political reasons his place was given to a Fleming, Jan Roettiers. Simon made his appeal against this decision in kind: the famous Petition Crown, in which he combined the subtle modelling of his Cromwell portraits with a decorative elegance calculated to please the new Court [figure 138]. But the issue was pre-judged and Roettiers kept his place, as perhaps he should have done, since the improvement in mechanical methods for which so many talented artists had worked, was in the end to favour mere competence at the expense of art.

For some years members of the Roettiers family were chief engravers at the mints of both London and Paris. The two establishments were very busy. In 1696 the London mint began

148 France, ½ écu aux palmes, c. 1694, overstruck
on a ½ écu aux 8 LL, Louis XIV; an example of
Louis's *réformations*, with the design and legend of the
earlier issue showing through plainly [actual size].

to recoin all the hammered silver issued before 1663. Five
provincial mints were set up as auxiliaries and the task was
completed in two years, James Roettiers' staff in London engraving all the dies. The Paris mint was kept active by recoinage
of a different kind. As a way out of his financial embarrass-
ments, Louis XIV resorted to the expedient of successive *réformations* of the coinage. The technique was to issue coins at an in-
flated tariff, rating the écu, for example, at 66 sous, to cry them
down by successive edicts to 60 sous, then to call them in,
recoin them with a new design and reissue them at the original
price, netting a profit of 10 per cent less minting expenses. To
reduce these expenses the coins were not always even melted
down, but were just overstruck so that the old design showed
through [figure 148]. The process was repeated five times between 1689 and 1715. It happened again in the early years of
Louis XV, when a *réformation* associated with the ministry of
the Duc de Noailles taxed the public at as much as 20 per cent;

149 England, silver crown, 1658,
Oliver Cromwell; a work of the
English medallist, Thomas Simon
[actual size].

150 Russia, silver rouble, Peter the
Great (1689-1725); the coinage was
one of the Russian institutions
which Peter reformed on western
models [actual size].

151 Sweden, silver riksdaler, 1707, Charles XII [actual size].

This Standard comixed of XXII Carretts of Fine Gold and II Carretts of Allay in the Pound w^t Troy of Great — Brittain made the 25th of June, 1707.

152 English gold trial plate of the reign of Queen Anne, stamped with the reverse die of a guinea of 1707; as this plate was in fact above standard, the Pyx jury of 1710 insisted on returning the verdict that the coin of the realm was deficient.

as if the Treasury today were to call in all ten-pence pieces and give only seven pence for them (or twenty cents for a quarter). It was no wonder in these circumstances that the Roettiers were content to keep their die-engraving to a level of mere competence.

A more genuine and thorough-going reform was undertaken in Russia at this time under the direction of Peter the Great. Machinery was installed at the Moscow mint and the rouble was devalued and transformed into a silver coin like the German thaler [figure 150]. Meanwhile in Germany itself the different 'circles' were engaged in the perennial task of trying to establish some sort of common standard which would fit the three different accounting systems. A series of conventions were agreed, but there were always important states such as Prussia which stood aloof, so the arrangements were never all-embracing. Moreover they were always liable to be upset by any change in the relative value of gold and silver or by inflation proceeding more rapidly in one part of the Empire than in another. Nevertheless something was achieved in that much of the coinage was made to fit the accounting system of the *gulden* in the Rhineland and the South, that of the thaler in Saxony and the North-west and that of the mark which still obtained in the North-east beyond the Elbe. It resulted, however, in German denominations being expressed in a bewildering variety of fractions and multiples, one gulden being equivalent to 24 *mariengroschen* (two-thirds of a thaler) by one system and two marks by the other.

153–155 Great Britain, copper, 1717, obverse; Ireland, copper 1722; British North America, copper, 1723, reverse. Three halfpence of George I, the last two issued for British dependencies by Mr Wood under royal patent. Because the Irish, inflamed by Dean Swift, rejected the coins, Wood was constrained to transfer his operations to the American colonies [actual size].

156 An eighteenth-century engraving of a screw-press in operation.

157 Great Britain copper twopence, 1797, George III; an early product of the Industrial Revolution, struck by Matthew Boulton's steam-press at Birmingham [actual size].

158 Macclesfield, copper halfpenny, 1791; one of the many English tokens issued privately at the end of the eighteenth century to relieve the shortage of small change [actual size].

The profusion of detail characteristic of German seventeenth-century coins gave way a little under French and Italian influence, but as if to make up for their restraint, the engravers took to crowding the legends. The awarding of titles was a much overworked instrument of imperial policy at this time and it became fashionable to string together as many as possible in a series of cryptic abbreviations. The legend on coins of the Elector Palatine Charles Theodore (1742–99) ran to as many as fifty initials. In 1714 George I brought this undiscriminating habit to England, where his royal titles were almost squeezed out by his arch-treasurership of the Holy Roman Empire.

Titles were left out on the English copper coinage, and on the halfpence and farthings of George I the simple legends do not distract the eye from a bust which, in its heavy dignity, is one of the best eighteenth-century evocations of the Roman style [figure 153]. Britannia on the reverse has a more direct classical pedigree, for she was adapted from a figure which had appeared on a sestertius of Antoninus Pius [figure 63]. Frances Stewart, later Duchess of Richmond, was reputed to have sat for the figure when it was first modelled for the copper coinage of Charles II in 1672.

The Irish coinage at this time was issued under a royal patent which had been bought by a hardware dealer called William Wood. It had none of the artistic quality of the English copper, but it was not on this ground that the Irish refused to take it. In his *Drapier's Letters*, Dean Swift seized on the patent as being typical of the English exploitation of Ireland. 'This abominable Project of Mr Wood', he argued, was even worse than the French *réformations*. 'For the French give their subjects *Silver* for *Silver* and *Gold* for *Gold*; but this *Fellow* will not give us good *Brass* or *Copper* for our *Gold* and *Silver*, nor even a twelfth Part of their Worth.' Wood was finally obliged to ship his coin to America, the inhabitants of which were at that time more biddable. At first the stuff was not even recoined, but Wood later adopted a new design for the American coin, a crowned rose and the legend *Rosa Americana*.

Swift's justifiable attack on a disreputable patent was coupled with a total misrepresentation of the nature of token coinage. Although the French had established copper coinage as the medium of small change in 1575, and the English, with rather more difficulty, in 1672, *Drapier's Letters* in 1724 could still appeal to deep-rooted public suspicion of the fiduciary principle. However, this was only four years after the South Sea Bubble in England and the collapse of Law's system in France, and financial experiment was understandably suspect.

Although the South Sea Company, in a later and more tranquil phase, supplied some silver to the mint, which marked the coins accordingly, the Bubble burst with no repercussions on the coinage. Law's scheme, by contrast, was a matter of public finance and it resulted in some radical alterations to the coinage; indeed Law came near to abolishing coinage altogether, nullified contracts stipulating payment in it and restricted its issue to two new minor denominations in silver, one in gold and small change in copper. Six years of financial chaos followed Law's collapse, but in 1726 Cardinal Fleury's government stabilized the louis at 24 livres and the écu at 6 livres, and so they stood until the Revolution, despite the later financial difficulties of the monarchy. As a mark of this new-found stability, the basic designs were kept virtually unchanged.

The later French coinage was typical of that of Europe: on the obverse a competent, rather flattering, portrait of the king, and on the reverse a traditional heraldic design, the whole not without a certain rococo elegance, but dull. A few coins stand out. One is the thaler of Frederick the Great of Prussia with its reverse design of a crowned eagle on a pile of standards, kettledrums and other military paraphernalia [figure 159]. Another is the rouble of Catherine the Great, whose harsh uncompromising portrait is very striking; it is a pity however that the tsarina's generous embonpoint wears unflatteringly in its bold relief. In England, the Industrial Revolution brought not only fresh imagery in coin design but also the new steam-press for better and more efficient striking. A shortage of small change in 1789 led to the unauthorized issue of a quantity of private tokens, many of which show figures emblematic of the new industries [figure 158] or vignettes of life in the factories of the issuing companies. However, the most magnificent early product of the steam-press was the official issue of twopenny and penny pieces, made in 1797 by the Birmingham manufacturer Matthew Boulton under government contract. The bust of George III on these coins, despite its light relief, has an impressive monumentality [figure 157]. On the reverse, Britannia, set for the first time amid the waves, is rather enhanced by the Union Jack on her shield, her trident and her man o' war, patriotic details suited to the first year in which England faced revolutionary France alone.

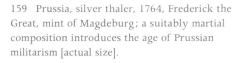

159 Prussia, silver thaler, 1764, Frederick the Great, mint of Magdeburg; a suitably martial composition introduces the age of Prussian militarism [actual size].

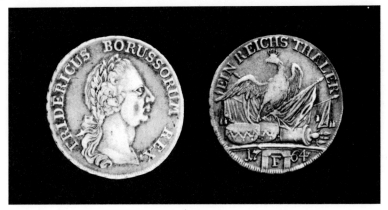

COINAGE TRANSFORMED

AMONG THE MANY SOCIAL CHANGES which followed the Industrial Revolution in England and the political revolutions in America and France, was a complete transformation of coinage. National currencies were successively reorganized on the decimal system. In 1785 Thomas Jefferson proposed in Congress a decimal coinage based on the dollar. The international currency of the New World and indeed of much of Europe at that time was provided by the Spanish dollar, and it was natural for the United States to base their own issue on a coin of the same weight and standard. The new system was established by the Coinage Act 1792: thenceforward the dollar, from being a piece of eight *reales,* became a piece of a hundred *cents.*

In 1794 the French Republic, following the American example, abolished the livre tournois and replaced it by the franc, a unit of value fixed in terms of both gold and silver and divisible into the *décime* and the *centime.* In France, however, the older methods of reckoning died hard: for more than a century the five centime piece was known in common speech as a sou, and the five franc piece alternatively as an écu or *pièce de cent sous.*

In the latter half of the nineteenth century decimalization spread rapidly, as it was adopted by the newly constituted nation-states of Europe and South America. In 1865 Belgium, Switzerland and Italy joined France in forming the Latin Monetary Union, whereby a common currency system was established between them. They were later joined by Greece and Spain [figure 165]. A uniform currency for Germany, based on the mark of one hundred pfennigs, was imposed in 1873: a concession was made to old traditions in the retention of both the thaler and the gulden in the form of the three-mark and two-mark pieces. The Netherlands and the Scandinavian countries decimalized in 1875, the Austro-Hungarian Empire in 1892 and Russia in 1897. Canada had adopted the American system in 1857 and from 1866 dollars of one hundred cents were issued by the British government for trade in the Far East. Nevertheless, in general the British Empire resisted the new trend. It is only in the last few years that the Commonwealth countries and Great Britain have successively adopted the decimal system. Rapid

160 One of the processes of a modern mint: annealed blanks being pickled, cleaned and washed in rotary drums at the Royal Mint, London.

162 Mexico, silver 8 reales, 1762, Charles III of Spain; the eighteenth-century dollar of the New World from which the US dollar was derived [actual size].

inflation in the 1960's had made coinage reform imperative in any case, and even British public opinion was finally reconciled to changing the time-honoured system.

The extensive currency reforms of the nineteenth century were not the only transformations which took place in that period. The primary purpose of coinage had of course always been to serve as the means of exchange, but as the demands of a growing industrial economy became more exacting, all other considerations were gradually excluded. Bearing the titles of rulers and the names of sovereign states, coins still reflected constitutional and political developments, but it was no longer more than a reflection. More effective means of communication and expression were available, while coins, passing more rapidly from hand to hand, were looked at less than before. Meanwhile the technical developments which enabled the demands on coinage to be met, had the effect of putting the artist at a greater distance from the final interpretation of his work. The reducing machine in particular [figure 174], which enabled one model to be used to produce an unlimited number of dies of different sizes, destroyed the sense of scale in relief which had distinguished the best coins of the past. Worst of all, coin design came under the dead hand of committee selection. The neo-classical fervour of revolutionary days was soon burnt out, but any departure in later years from the academic conventions which it left behind was rarely approved.

In the nineteenth century coinage at least kept its primary rôle of providing the money-supply of nations. Its importance, however, was progressively diminished as more money was created by the mechanisms of public and private credit and in this century it has become mere small change. Gold disappeared

161 (opposite) This steam coining press was made in Barcelona in 1856; powered by the first steam engine to be used in Spain, its operating speed was 40 rpm.

83

164 *(right)* Great Britain, crown, 1818, George III; designed by Benedetto Pistrucci, a protégé of the Prince Regent. The George and Dragon reverse is still used on the gold sovereign [enlarged 3:1].

163 *(right)* USA, copper cent, 1793; the first coin issued by the United States under the Coinage Act, 1792, by the Swiss designer Droz [actual size].

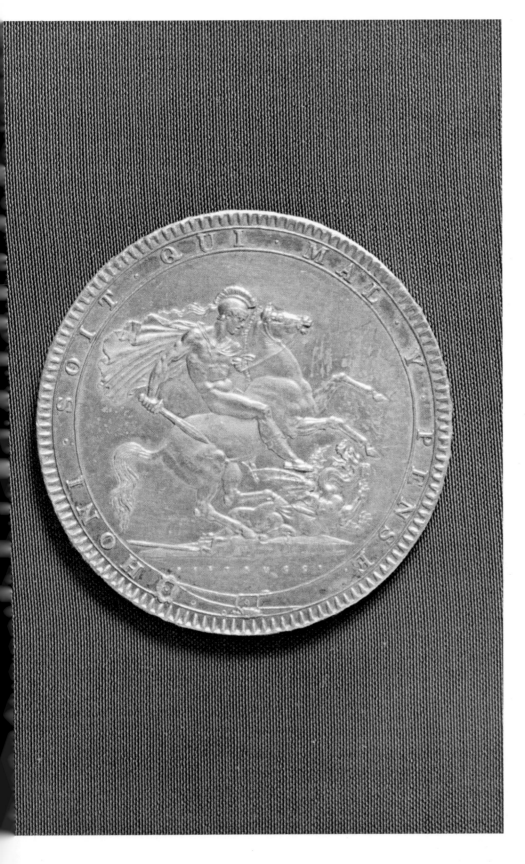

165 Spain, silver peseta, 1894, Alfonso XIII, reverse; a typical coin of the Latin Monetary Union [actual size].

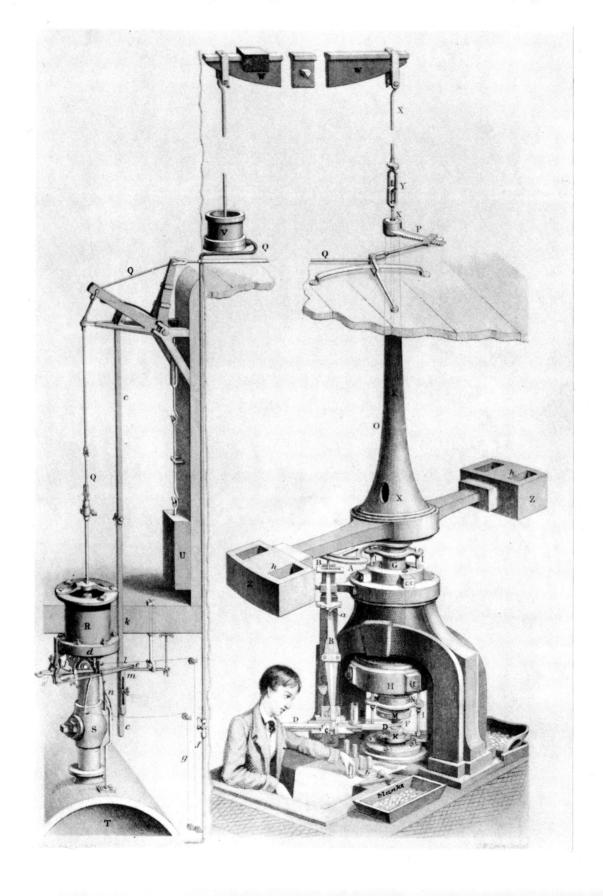

86

167 Switzerland, nickel 20 centimes, 1881, mint of Berne; the first coin to be made of pure nickel [twice actual size].

166 *(opposite)* Steel engraving of the Bolton screw-press, from Ansell's *Treatise on Coinage,* 1862.

from currency as a result of the First World War, and in the succeeding years most countries debased their silver. The seeds of this second development were sown paradoxically in Switzerland, the only European country to preserve its silver coinage intact in 1964. In 1881, after experimenting with various alloys, the Confederation chose nickel as the material for its coins in the lower-middle range of values [figure 167]. Alloyed with copper, this metal had been used for Bactrian coins of *c.* 150 BC, but the discovery of large deposits in Canada provided governments with a new and attractive coinage material. Its use was confined at first to those values for which silver was too precious, but which it was inconvenient to mint in copper or bronze, such as the American five-cent piece to which it gives its name. Post-war inflation extended its range to such coins as the French five-franc piece and the Italian lira, as it was generally taken as the best white metal substitute for silver. Just how much the best was demonstrated during the two World Wars, when nickel and copper, rare strategic materials, were replaced by iron and aluminium in many European coinages. Most depressing of all were the zinc coins, which, drab grey as the Wehrmacht itself, spread through the occupied territories from 1941 [figure 168].

In both wars Great Britain was spared an *ersatz* coinage, but in 1920 the silver coinage had to be debased by 50 per cent, and in 1948 it was discontinued altogether. The silver in circulation was melted down and sent to America as repayment under the Lend Lease agreement, and cupronickel coins of the same size

168 *(left)* The Netherlands, zinc 20 cents, 1941; *(right)* Norway, iron 5 øre, 1943. During the Second World War the Germans used these two metals for coinage in occupied countries [actual size].

169 USA, gold quarter 'eagle' ($2\frac{1}{2}$ dollars), 1908; a modern coin whose name derives from its type, after the manner of the 'turtles' and 'colts' of ancient Greece [twice actual size].

170 *(right)* The raw materials of modern coinage: an ingot of copper, raw nickel and scrap French 100-franc pieces for melting down at the Royal Mint,.London.

171 Kingdom of Holland, silver 2½ gulden, Louis Napoleon (1806-10); a typical coin of the Napoleonic period [actual size].

172 Principate of Lucca and Piombino, silver 5 francs, 1808, Felice and Elisa Baciocchi; some of the best neo-classical designs came from the Napoleonic states of Italy [actual size].

173 Kingdom of the Two Sicilies, bronze 5 centesimi, 1813, Joachim Murat; the romantic portrait of Murat stands out as exceptional among the austere neo-classicism of most Napoleonic coins [actual size].

and weight were issued instead. One result of this was that British coins, although base-metal, retained the constant weight-value relationship of silver coins. This was convenient for banks and the operators of slot machines, but when inflation had reduced the purchasing power of the biggest coin in circulation to that of a sixpence in 1900, it stood in the way of reform. What was needed were smaller but higher-value coins such as were issued in most European countries, where coinage had been adapted to its new rôle of providing token small change in convenient amounts. The size of gold and silver coins is automatically reduced by inflation, but if a weight-value relationship is strictly upheld for a token coinage, the logical result of inflation is the issue of bigger and bigger lumps of base metal. Coinage reform, when it came to Great Britain with decimalization in 1971, did meet this problem.

A detailed examination of the mass-produced coinage of the last hundred and seventy years is outside the scope of this book, but among the quantities of material there are coins, and indeed whole series of coins, of distinction. It is, however, surprising how often what at first appears to be an exceptionally good, even original, design, turns out to be derived from an ancient prototype. Neo-classicism was of course the natural artistic expression of revolutionary America and France [figures 163 and 176]. As in their constitutional forms, so in their new coinage, the United States resorted to the imagery of republican Rome, and a bust of Liberty was chosen as the type for the new dollars and cents of 1792 [figure 163]. The portraiture of dead statesmen, which has more recently been a feature of American coin types, is another idea borrowed from Rome. American engravers have remained very faithful to these conventional republican motives but, as the neo-classicism in which they are rooted has dried up artistically, the designs have become progressively more banal. Specifically American types, such as the Indian heads on the half and quarter 'eagles' of 1908 and on the nickel of 1912, have generally been more successful [figure 169].

In France the National Assembly held a public competition in 1791 to produce dies for a new coinage, and Augustin Dupré, adjudged the winner by the painter David, was appointed engraver-general. Dupré's first designs, as required by the Assembly's decree, were a faithful expression of the spirit of the Constitution of 1791, which indeed appeared personified on the reverse, inscribing a tablet [figure 176]. The new portrait of the king was shorn of majesty, the simple legend, *Louis XVI Roi des François*, replaced the Latin titles, and two statements of political principle were substituted for the sacred texts of the old coinage.

Dupré's constitutional coinage was later adapted to the needs of the First Republic by the elimination of the king's name and portrait, but new designs were called for in 1794 when the cur-

174 A modern reducing machine at the Royal Mint, London; this reproduces the large-scale plaster model on the right (in this instance the reverse of an English half-crown) on a steel punch of the required size.

rency was changed. The first coins issued under the new system were copper décimes and five-centime pieces. Dupré's design for these early expressed the change in mood since 1791. The fierce young woman in her phrygian cap was a fit emblem, if not of the Reign of Terror, at least of the militant spirit of France; as such indeed she was revived briefly for use in besieged Strasbourg after the fall of the Second Empire in 1870.

Just as the First Republic had consciously imitated the forms of republican Rome, so Napoleon's coinage, superficially at least, copied the Augustan pattern. His first coins, designed in 1798 by Tiolier, carried a simple head, bare of all ornament and essentially civilian in character [figure 175]. For all its simplicity, however, this portrait differed strongly from that of Louis XVI which had appeared seven years earlier on the constitutional coinage. The king had been represented, not without pathos, as plain Louis Capet; the First Consul was shown as embodying already a universal imperial ideal, the successor, indeed, not so much of Augustus as of Constantine.

In earlier centuries a monotonous repetition of the same types had masked the steady depreciation of the French coinage; in the nineteenth century the weight and fineness of the coins remained constant, but there was a change of type for every shift in the political scene. These changes formed a pattern which was variously followed by the other European countries throughout this period of political experiment and change. For Napoleon as emperor, Tiolier's portrait was recast in a more heroic mould, larger and with a laurel wreath. At the Restoration, a crowned

175 France, silver 5 francs, Bonaparte First Consul (1799-1804); this fine profile, engraved by Pierre Joseph Tiolier, was intended to recall the coin portraiture of Augustus [actual size].

176 France écu constitutionel, 1792, Louis XVI, Paris; the first coins of the French Revolution, designed by Augustin Dupré [twice actual size].

shield of the arms of France and the old title of *Roi de France* were revived as features of a legitimist coinage, only to be removed again after the July Revolution. A civic crown of oak leaves distinguished Louis Philippe on most of his coins from the laureate emperor and the bare-headed Bourbons, presumably an obscure allusion to his own bourgeois strain of kingship; the

177 Great Britain, silver shilling,
1826, George IV; engraved by William Wyon
after a bust by Chantrey [enlarged $1\frac{1}{2}$: 1].

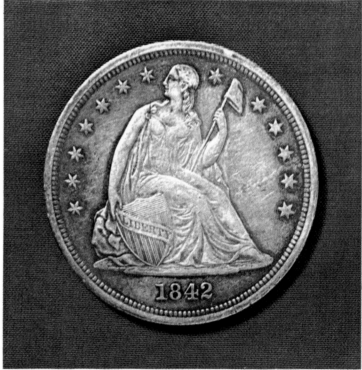

178 USA, silver dollar, 1842; designed by
Christian Gobrecht in 1836, this was one of the
last successful coins in the neo-classical idiom
[twice actual size].

fashion was adopted by other constitutional kings, notably
Leopold I of the Belgians in 1832.

For the Second Republic, a number of Dupré's designs were
reconstituted, but by 1848 the fashion was for Greek rather than
Roman art, and a new design for the silver, a head of Ceres by
Oudiné, was copied from a Siculo-Punic coin of 240 BC. The

93

179 *(above, left)* Ghana, cupronickel threepence, 1958, President Nkrumah; engraved by Paul Vincze, this is a notable modern portrait coin from the Royal Mint, London [enlarged 3:1].

180 *(above, right)* Great Britain, nickel brass threepence, 1961, Elizabeth II, reverse. British coin design has been very conservative in recent years; this, designed by William Gardner, is one of the most successful examples [enlarged 3:1].

choice of a Carthaginian model may have reflected French aspirations in North Africa at the time. It was popular and had a long life, since, although Louis Napoleon replaced it by a portrait of himself in 1851, it was revived after the fall of the Second Empire in 1870 and was used on both silver and bronze until 1890.

The style of the first Napoleon's coinage spread from France over Europe with his military conquests. In Spain, the Netherlands and parts of Germany, Joseph, Louis and Jerôme Bonaparte palely reflected the image of their imperial brother [figure 171]; the romantic bravura of the portrait of the King of Naples, Napoleon's son-in-law Joachim Murat [figure 173], stands out as exceptional in this austere family group.

Some of the best designs in the neo-classical idiom were done for the Napoleonic states of Italy [figure 172], and it was an Italian, Benedetto Pistrucci, who was chosen by the Prince Regent to engrave the new English coinage which was called for after the Napoleonic wars. The wars had been fought largely on paper money and Spanish dollars, countermarked and later recoined by the Bank of England, but in 1816 the government abandoned bimetallism for the gold standard and issued a complete new coinage in gold and silver. The new issue was distinguished for Pistrucci's fine series of portrait heads of the aged George III, but the most memorable of his designs was the George and Dragon which he adapted from an antique cameo for the reverse type of the gold sovereign and the silver crown [figure

182 William Wyon (1795–1851), a drawing by
W. Brockedon; the Wyon family dominated
English die-engraving during the greater part of
the nineteenth century.

181 Pierre Joseph Tiolier, Graveur Général
des Monnaies Françaises during the reign of
Napoleon.

164]. With its energetic circular rhythm it is one of the most successful of modern coin designs. Its popularity led to its revival in 1870 for the gold coinage of Queen Victoria, and its association thereafter with the sovereign in its heyday as an international currency turned it into a kind of symbol of the immutability of the gold standard and of sterling worth. It is now the badge of the England cricket team.

Pistrucci was regarded as an intruder on the preserve of the Wyon family which at that time dominated English die-engraving. Some of their work was of great delicacy: a head of George IV [figure 177], after a bust by Chantrey, and the young head of Victoria, both by William Wyon, and later, by L.C. Wyon, the bust of Victoria on the bronze 'bun' penny of 1860. This portrait somewhat flattered the queen, then in her fortieth year, but it was very popular and persisted until she was seventy-three.

Some of the coins issued at the end of the century in London, Birmingham and Bombay for various parts of the British Empire, carrying the message 'Rule Britannia!' to the queen's oriental subjects, were perhaps a late exception to the principle that coins in recent years have ceased to express any particular political idea. As such they deserve mention, but the weakness of their relief detracts sadly from such merits as there may be in the composition. The last really effective British coin was the vast head of Edward VII, one of the triumphs of the reducing machine, as it dominates every coin from the crown [figure 184] to the Maundy penny. More recently the committees have done their work only too well, but if the British coins, with a few exceptions [figure 180], are lamentable, the Royal Mint at least

183 Free City of Danzig,
nickel 10 gulden (obverse and
reverse) and, centre, 5 gulden
(reverse), 1935; two of the rare
examples of fine coin design
in the twentieth century [actual
size].

is not to blame for them. It competes for business in the world market, and has some good coins to its credit, the coinage of Ireland, for example, although the best design there comes straight from the tetradrachm of Thurium [figure 25], and a portrait of President Nkrumah of Ghana by Paul Vincze, which recalls, perhaps deliberately, some of the Roman emperors of the third century [figure 179]. As one might expect, however, the best modern design has come from northern Europe and Scandinavia. Some coins of the free city of Danzig [figure 183], and more recently a portrait of King Gustav VI of Sweden, both in a twentieth-century idiom, prove that coinage can still achieve distinction in a city-state or under the critical eye of an artistic monarch.

184 Great Britain, silver crown, 1902,
Edward VII [actual size].